Jean Humphrey
Honolulu
May, 1984

CLEANING & COOKING FISH

THE HUNTING & FISHING LIBRARY

Golden Press · New York

Western Publishing Company, Inc.

Racine, Wisconsin

By Sylvia Bashline

SYLVIA BASHLINE is the Food Editor for *Field & Stream* magazine. She has won several awards for her articles and photos dealing with a variety of outdoor subjects. She has served as president of the Pennsylvania Outdoor Writers Association, and is currently on the board of directors of Outdoor Writers Association of America.

Sylvia has roasted brook trout over a campfire in Maine, panfried crappies in a Kentucky campground, barbecued largemouth bass on a Texas ranch, and poached lake trout in the wilds of Saskatchewan, all while gathering information for her books and magazine articles.

She lives with husband, Jim Bashline, a noted outdoor writer, and their Labrador retriever, Shadow, in a wooded corner of Chester County, Pennsylvania.

CREDITS:
Author: Sylvia Bashline
Project Director: Dick Sternberg
Editor: Mary Ann Knox
Editorial Director: Chuck Wechsler
Design and Production: Cy DeCosse Creative Department, Inc.
Art Directors: Cy DeCosse, Delores Swanson
Production Coordinators: Julia Slott, Christine Watkins
Photographers: Graham Brown, Buck Holzemer, Steve McHugh
Food Stylists: Lynn Lohmann, Susan Zechmann
Home Economists: Jill Crum, Peggy Lamb, Kathy Weber
Typesetter: Ellen Sorenson
Consultants: Joanne Crocker, Jim Schneider
Color Separations: Weston Engraving Co., Inc.
Printing: Moebius Printing Co.

Also available from the publisher: *The Art of Freshwater Fishing* by Dick Sternberg.

Produced in the U.S.A.
Library of Congress Catalog Card Number:
 82-80889
Golden® and Golden Press® are trademarks of
 Western Publishing Company, Inc.
ISBN 0-307-46631-0

Contents

Introduction

Fishermen throughout North America are catching and bringing home more fish than ever before. And their catch is no longer just bass, panfish, walleyes and the like. The modern angler is also catching salmon, striped bass and other gamefish introduced in freshwater lakes and reservoirs.

With the ever-growing variety of gamefish, along with ever-increasing grocery bills, it pays to become more versatile in all phases of fish cookery.

The first section in this book features the different methods and equipment you need to keep your catch in top condition until it reaches the cleaning table. Step-by-step photographs and instructions guide you through the various cleaning methods, from field dressing and filleting to more involved techniques for cleaning catfish and removing Y bones from northern pike.

The second section acquaints cooks with all of the popular methods for cooking fish. Nutritionists make a sound case for more fish in our diets. But fish can be boring if it is always prepared the same way. Many youngsters grew up thinking that fish is always fried. Many of these people dislike the taste of fish; that is, until they try it by another method.

Close-up photographs show numerous shortcuts and tips to help you master the various cooking techniques, from baking to poaching to smoke-cooking. Each method is complemented by a cooking chart to help you retain the natural flavor of fish. Prepared by home economists, the charts recommend ideal cooking times for different types of fish. Of special interest to novice cooks are photos showing how to present fish attractively at the table.

In the third section, the cook is led into a new world of cooking and eating adventures. Recipes cover everything from appetizers, salads, soups and chowders to main dishes such as stuffed fish, casseroles and omelets.

The last section contains easy directions for making exotic-sounding dishes such as seviche and gravlax, as well as procedures for canning and pickling fish. These preserving techniques are not complicated, and all can be done easily at home.

While this book is primarily for the family that catches its own fish, it can be helpful for the cook who buys fish at the store. Many gamefish, including walleyes, lake trout, rainbow trout, catfish, northern pike and perch, are sold over the counter.

Whether you purchase trout from the grocery store or catch a basket of bluegills from your favorite pond, this book provides all of the basic information you need to successfully clean and cook your fish.

Initial Care

Fish are extremely perishable. Fish that do not have red gills, clear eyes and a fresh odor should be discarded. Proper care insures firm flesh for cooking.

The secret to preserving your catch is to keep it alive or cold. If the surface water is cool, a stringer or wire basket can keep some fish species alive. Bring the fish aboard when moving the boat to a new spot. Return them to the water as soon as possible.

Check your catch often, whether the fish are on a stringer, in a wire basket or live well. Transfer dead

WIRE BASKETS or net bags hung over the side of the boat keep small fish alive. The fish should have ample room to move around.

AERATED LIVE WELLS in many boats keep bass, northern pike and other hardy fish alive. Limit the number of fish; remove dead ones to ice immediately.

CLIP-TYPE STRINGERS are preferable to the rope style because fish are not crowded. However, rope stringers are better for very large fish.

ones to an ice-filled cooler immediately. Dead fish left in water spoil rapidly.

Large gamefish should be killed immediately. Use a stout stick and rap the fish across the back of the head. Their flesh can bruise if they flop around in a boat. Field dress (page 8) as soon as possible and place the fish on ice.

Keeping fish in good condition on extended trips is difficult. Fish held longer than 2 days should be super-chilled (page 29), frozen or smoked. You can often take advantage of motel facilities to keep your catch cold or frozen. If shipping fish by plane, place them in a Styrofoam® cooler wrapped with a layer of heavy cardboard.

AVOID placing fish in the sunshine or in a non-porous wrapping such as a plastic bag or rubberized pouch. Fish spoil quickly without air circulation.

COOLERS filled with ice keep fish cold. Crushed ice chills fish faster than a solid block. Drain the cooler often so the catch does not soak in water.

WICKER CREELS are used by wading anglers. Place layers of moss, ferns or grass between the fish to provide ventilation. Transfer to ice as soon as possible.

BURLAP bags, newspapers, moss or materials that "breathe" help preserve fish when ice is not available. Keep the covering moist; evaporation helps cool fish.

Field Dressing

For top quality and flavor, fish should be field dressed as quickly as possible by removing the gills, guts and kidney, all of which spoil fast in a dead fish.

Field dress fish that are to be cooked whole or steaked. It is not necessary to field dress fish if they are to be filleted within an hour or two. Scale fish that are to be cooked with their skin on, but only if they have large scales. These fish include bluegills, perch, crappies, black bass, striped bass, walleyes, northern pike and large salmon.

When field dressing and scaling at home, place your catch on several layers of newspaper to ease cleanup. Before field dressing, wipe the fish with paper towels to remove slime. This makes it easier to hold the fish firmly. If you puncture the guts, wash the body cavity with cold water. Use water sparingly, because it softens the flesh.

The head can be removed after scaling. Paper towels are excellent for wiping off scales and blood spots, and for drying fish.

Field dressing is easier if you have the right tools, and if you clean the fish in a convenient location. Practice the different cleaning techniques until you can clean fish quickly and with little waste.

How to Field Dress Small Trout and Salmon

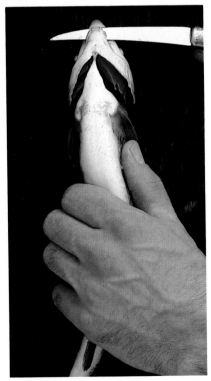  

SLICE the throat connection, the tissue that connects the lower jaw and the gill membrane.

INSERT the knife in the vent; run the blade tip up the stomach to the gills. Try not to puncture the intestines.

PUSH your thumb into the throat; pull gills and guts toward the tail. Scrape out the bloodline with a spoon.

SCALING fish is quick and easy with a scaler, though a dull knife or a spoon can be used. Wet the fish and scrape off the scales, working from tail to head. This job should be done outdoors, because scales fly in all directions. Or, line the kitchen sink with newspapers and scale as carefully as possible.

How to Field Dress Other Fish

  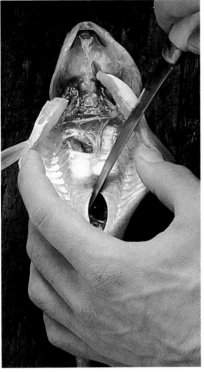

REMOVE gills by cutting the throat connection, then along both sides of the arch so the gills pull out easily.

INSERT the knife in the vent. Run the blade tip to the gills. Pull the guts and gills out of the cavity.

CUT the membrane along the backbone. Scrape out the kidney or bloodline underneath the membrane.

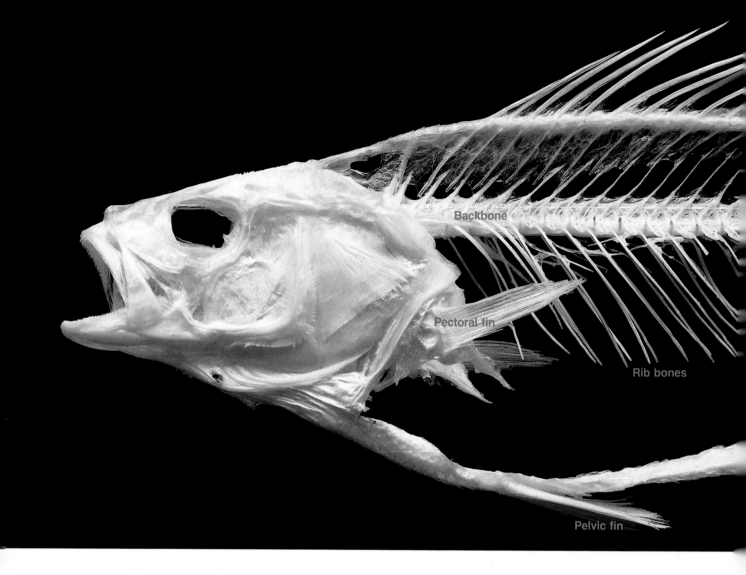

Backbone

Pectoral fin

Rib bones

Pelvic fin

The Art of Filleting

Filleting is the most common method of cleaning fish. It is easily mastered with a little practice and some knowledge of the bone structure and location of the various fins (above). The technique is popular because most of the flesh can be quickly removed from the bones without touching the intestines. In addition, the boneless fillets can be cooked in many ways and are easy to eat.

How to Select and Sharpen Fillet Knives

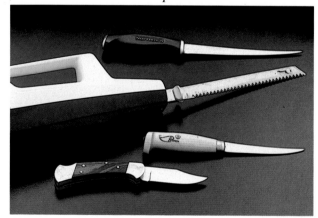

FILLETING is easiest with a thin, flexible knife. Some anglers, however, prefer a short, firm blade. Electric carving knives are also used.

REALIGN the cutting edge with a sharpening steel. Alternately draw each side of the blade *into* the steel at a 20- to 30-degree angle, about 10 strokes per side.

← Dorsal fins →

Caudal or Tail fin

Anal fin

A sharp knife is essential when filleting fish. Use a sharpening stone and steel to touch up knife blades. Fillet knives of hard steel will hold their edge longer than soft steel. However, soft steel requires less effort to sharpen. It is interesting and helpful to watch butchers sharpen and realign knives.

Ideally, the length of the blade should fit the fish. Because good fillet knives last many years, it pays to have two or three sizes. A wooden fillet board with a clip on one end is useful for holding fish. If outdoors, fillet your fish on an oar, paddle, or the lid of a plastic cooler.

SHARPEN a knife by pushing the blade into a honing stone, as if cutting a thin slice of stone. The blade should be at a 15- to 20-degree angle to the stone.

HONING OIL can be added to lubricate a stone, resulting in a finer cutting edge. Most stones have two sides, one coarse and the other fine texture.

Basic Filleting Technique

Fishermen use a variety of filleting techniques. The method shown below is the easiest and quickest for most anglers. Fillets can be stripped from the backbone in 30 seconds with a very sharp knife. Removing the rib bones takes a few additional seconds. Other methods are described on following pages.

If your fillet board does not have a clip, you can use a fork to pin the head of a small fish. A fork or pliers can also be useful during skinning. Salt on the hands helps hold a slippery fish.

The skin can be removed or left on. Fish such as largemouth bass have strong-tasting skin, so many anglers remove it. However, the skin on small trout and panfish is tasty. Panfish have large scales which must be removed if the skin is retained.

How to Fillet and Skin a Fish

LIFT the pectoral fin. Angle the knife towards the back of the head and cut to the backbone.

TURN the blade parallel to the backbone. Cut towards tail with a sawing motion. Cut fillet off.

REMOVE the rib bones by sliding the blade along the ribs. Turn fish over and remove second fillet.

Keep the skin on fillets that will be charcoal grilled. This helps prevent the flesh from falling apart, sticking to the grill and overcooking. Cut long fillets into serving-size pieces before they are cooked or stored. Thick fillets can be divided into two thin fillets for easier cooking.

Remove the thin strip of fatty belly flesh on oily fish such as salmon and large trout. Any contaminants will settle into this fatty tissue. To clean fillets, wipe with paper towels or rinse quickly under cold running water. Dry thoroughly with paper towels.

After filleting, rinse hands with clear water before using soap. Rub hands with vinegar and salt, lemon juice or toothpaste to remove the fishy smell.

Save the bones and head after filleting. These pieces can be used for stock, chowder, fish cakes or other dishes (page 78).

CUT off the strip of fatty belly flesh. Discard guts and belly. Save bones and head for stock.

SKIN the fillet, if desired, by cutting into the tail flesh to the skin. Turn the blade parallel to the skin.

PULL the skin firmly while moving the knife in a sawing action between the skin and the flesh.

13

Canadian Filleting Technique

Some fishermen find this technique easier than the basic method (page 12), especially when used on fish with a heavy rib structure such as white bass and large black bass. The Canadian technique takes a little longer and leaves more flesh on the bones. But many anglers are comfortable with this method,

How to Fillet Using the Canadian Technique

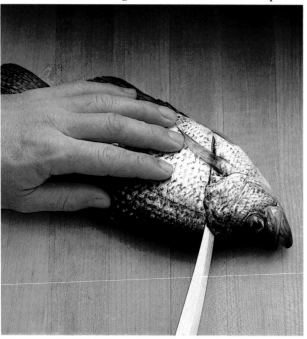

CUT behind the pectoral fin straight down to the backbone. Angle the cut towards the top of the head.

RUN the knife along one side of the backbone. The knife should scrape the rib bones without cutting them.

REMOVE the first boneless fillet by cutting through the skin of the stomach area.

TURN the fish over. Remove the second fillet using the same filleting technique.

because it eliminates the extra step of cutting the rib bones from the fillet. As a bonus, your knife stays sharp longer, because the boneless fillet is removed without cutting through the rib bones. Be careful when cutting the belly, so the knife does not penetrate the guts.

PUSH the knife through the flesh near the vent just behind the rib bones. Cut the fillet free at the tail.

CUT the flesh carefully away from the rib cage. To save flesh, the blade should graze the bones.

RINSE fillets quickly with cold water or wipe with paper towels. Save head and skeleton for stock (page 26).

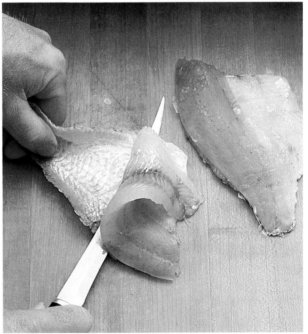

SKIN fillets, if desired. Hold the tail with your fingertips and cut between flesh and skin with a sawing motion.

Filleting With an Electric Knife

An electric knife is particularly useful for filleting panfish, catfish or any large fish that has heavy rib bones. Scale fish before filleting if the skin will be retained for cooking. Skin is usually removed from largemouth bass, striped bass, and other fish which have strong-tasting skin.

How to Fillet With an Electric Knife

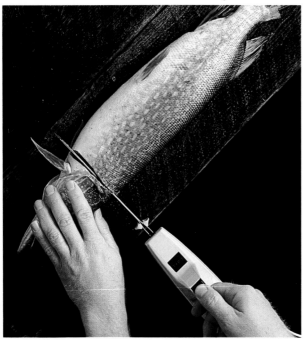

CUT behind the pectoral fin straight down to the backbone, holding the fish at the edge of the counter.

TURN the knife parallel to the backbone and cut toward the tail, firmly grasping the head.

AVOID cutting the fillet from the tail if skin is to be removed. Turn fillet over, hold the tail and begin the cut.

GUIDE the knife between skin and flesh. Remove rib bones with small knife. Turn fish; fillet other side.

Pan Dressing Fish

Panfish, including bluegills, crappies and yellow perch, are often too small for filleting. They are usually pan dressed instead. Scales, fins, guts and head are always removed. The tail is quite tasty and can be left on. Most of the tiny fin bones in a fish are removed by pan dressing.

How to Pan Dress Whole Fish

SLICE along the dorsal fin of the scaled panfish. Make the same cut on the other side, then pull out the fin.

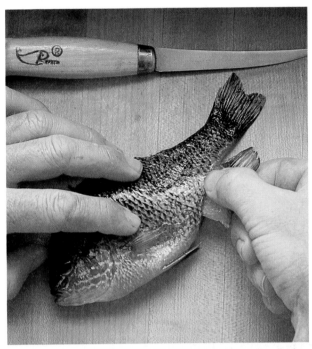

CUT along both sides of the anal fin. Remove the fin by pulling it towards the tail.

REMOVE the head. Angle the blade over the top of the head to save as much flesh as possible.

SLIT the belly and pull out the guts. Cut off tail, if desired. Rinse fish quickly; dry with paper towels.

Y Bones

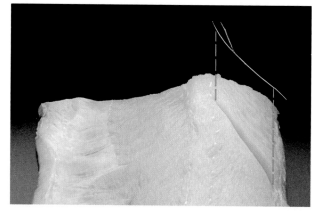

Northern pike, muskellunge and pickerel have a row of Y-shaped bones that float just above the ribs. The Y bones run lengthwise along the fillet, ending above the vent.

Many anglers remove Y bones before cooking, even though some flesh is lost when they are cut out. The alternative is to pull out the Y bones after cooking.

Y BONES lie within a narrow strip of flesh just above the rib cage.

How to Remove Y Bones

SLICE through the flesh along the edge of the Y bones (arrows). The fillet at left will be boneless.

CUT the flesh from the Y bones by guiding the knife blade along the bones (arrow), scraping lightly.

REMOVE the triangular strip of bones and flesh; save them for stock. Two long boneless fillets remain.

The Lateral Line

Some gamefish such as largemouth bass, striped bass, northern pike and white bass have a lateral line of strong-tasting flesh.

For cleaning and cooking purposes, the lateral line is defined as the band of dark-colored flesh along the side of a fish. It covers the entire side of some fish. This flesh spoils easily and develops an odor when the fish has been frozen too long.

In some species, such as trout and salmon, the lateral line does not have a strong flavor and may be retained. Many people enjoy the "fishy" taste of the lateral line. It is particularly flavorful when the fish is smoked or cooked and served cold.

Many anglers remove the lateral line if the fish are taken from waters of marginal quality. Contaminants tend to concentrate in the lateral line flesh.

How to Remove the Lateral Line

SKIN the fillet to expose the lateral line. In most species, it is an oily layer of reddish or brownish flesh.

CUT away the shallow band of dark flesh, using an extremely sharp fillet knife. Remove the lateral line; discard.

ANOTHER method is to tip the blade up while skinning so the lateral line is removed with the skin.

Cleaning Catfish & Bullheads

Catfish and bullheads are skinned regardless of size, which ranges from pan-size to over 70 pounds. The skin is thin and slippery, which demands a special skinning technique.

Cleaning and skinning requires a wide-jawed pliers, a sharp knife, and sometimes, a board with a nail to hold the head in place. Many anglers improvise. Fish can be hand-held instead of impaled on a nail. Fishermen's or regular pliers can be used.

The technique for skinning small catfish and bullheads is a little different from that used for larger catfish. Two popular methods are described below and on the next page.

Catfish or bullheads smaller than 10 inches long are cooked whole after skinning. Larger fish are filleted, steaked or chunked. Thick fillets from extremely large catfish can be sliced into thinner fillets that can be cooked easily.

How to Clean Bullheads and Small Catfish

GRIP the head tightly, taking care to avoid the *horns* or pectoral spines. Cut just behind the head.

SLICE the skin cleanly along the backbone to a point just behind the dorsal fin. The fish is now ready for skinning.

GRASP the skin with the pliers and pull it all the way to the tail. Repeat the process on the other side.

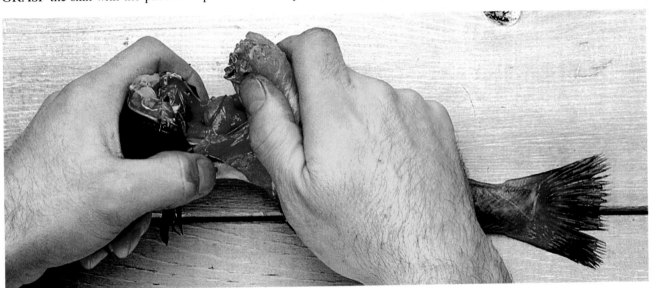

BEND the head downward until the backbone snaps. The head and guts will tear away from the flesh.

CUT along both sides of the dorsal and anal fins. Pull out both fins with the pliers. Slice off the tail.

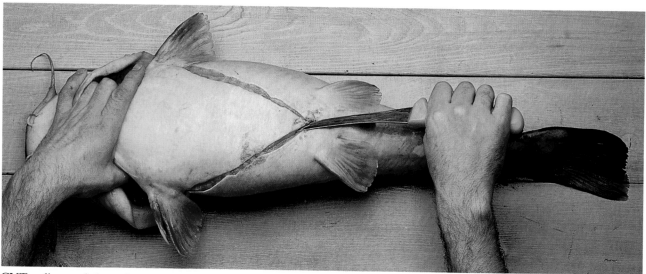

CUT a diamond-shaped pattern on the belly. The cut should slice the skin from the pectoral spines to the pelvic fins.

TURN the fish onto its belly. Cut behind the head, extending down the sides to the diamond cut behind the pectoral spines.

SLICE the skin, beginning at the cut behind the head and continuing to a point just behind the dorsal fin.

GRASP the skin with the pliers. Pull with a sharp jerk. Remove one side at a time. Grasp the skin again if it tears.

FLOP the fish. Grasp the skin at the back of the diamond-shaped cut. Yank the belly skin toward the head.

SEVER the backbone with a heavy knife or cleaver and a hammer. Remove the fins (page 21) and guts.

Steaking Large Fish

Gamefish of 6 pounds or more *can* be steaked. Fish over 15 pounds *should* be steaked or chunked, so they are easier to cook. Before steaking, scale fish that have large scales. Then, remove the guts, kidney (bloodline) and dorsal fin. Rinse in cold running water and wipe with paper towels.

Partially frozen fish are easier to cut into steaks. Firm up the flesh by super-chilling (page 29) or by placing them in a freezer until they begin to stiffen.

Lay the fish on its side. Use a sharp knife to cut even, ¾- to 1-inch thick steaks from the fish. Cut through the backbone with a sturdy knife, electric knife, kitchen saw or frozen-food knife. After steaking, trim fatty belly flesh from oily fish such as salmon, trout or striped bass.

The tail sections of large gamefish can be left whole, filleted or cut into 1½- to 2-inch chunks for baking or smoking. Save the head to make stock (page 26).

Tips for Steaking Fish

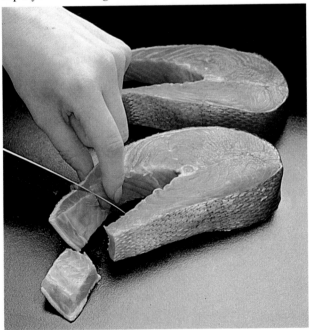

TRIM and throw away pieces of fatty belly flesh from the ends of the steaks.

FILLET the tail section by sliding a sharp knife along the backbone in a sawing motion.

Using All of the Fish

Some flesh remains on fish bones and head after filleting and steaking. Don't waste it. Make a fish stock by simmering the skeleton and the head. They add rich flavor to the stock.

The flaked cooked fish can be used for fish chowder, quiche, salad, cakes, loaf, patties or sandwich spread. (See recipe section.) Store the fish in plastic containers in the refrigerator for no longer than 2 days, or in the freezer for no longer than 2 weeks.

Use the remaining fish stock as a foundation for chowder, sauces or soups. Refrigerate or freeze the stock. Fish stock frozen in 1- or 2-cup quantities is the easiest to thaw. Instructions for thawing in a microwave oven are on page 59.

There are other uses for whole heads or backbones. Smoke or bake a cleaned fish head. Coat a meaty backbone with flour and panfry. Or, brush it with barbecue sauce and grill. The slabs of cheek meat, located just below the eyes on large gamefish, are tasty. Remove with a knife tip and panfry in butter.

How to Remove Flesh and Make Fish Stock

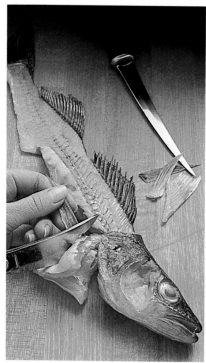

REMOVE the guts, gills, fins and tail, after cutting out the cheeks (top photo). Use a kitchen shears or sharp knife. Scale the head, if necessary.

RINSE the head under cold running water. Wipe off slime with paper towels. Cut the skeleton into small pieces that fit easily into the pan.

COVER the skeleton with water. Add a dash of salt and pepper. Heat to boiling; reduce heat. Simmer for 30 minutes. Remove head and bones.

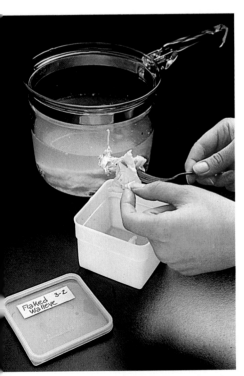

STRIP the cooked flesh from the bones and head; discard the bones. Freeze or refrigerate the flaked fish in plastic containers or freezer bags.

STRAIN the cooked fish stock through a double layer of cheesecloth to remove any remaining bones and scales. Return stock to pan.

BOIL the stock over high heat to reduce it by half for storage; cool. Freeze or refrigerate in plastic containers. Label as fish stock.

Storing Fish

For top flavor, clean and cook your gamefish within 2 hours after catching it. However, most anglers have to keep their catch for a longer time.

The colder the storage temperature, the longer the fish can be held. If handled and cleaned properly, fish can be refrigerated for 24 hours with little flavor loss. Fish stored on crushed ice will remain fresh for 2 or 3 days, but they must be drained often. Super-chilled fish can be kept up to 7 days.

Lean fish can be stored longer than oily fish; whole fish longer than fillets or steaks.

To prepare fish for storing, wipe with paper towels. Rinse in cold water if intestines were penetrated during cleaning.

Super-chilling is storing fish on crushed ice, and covering them with a salt-ice mixture. This method holds fish at about 28°, which is a colder temperature than refrigeration. It is especially helpful on long trips when freezing facilities are not available.

Wrap whole fish, fillets or steaks in aluminum foil or plastic wrap before super-chilling. As the ice melts, add more of the salt-ice mixture.

How to Refrigerate Fish

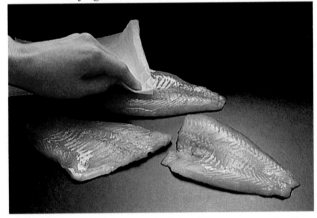

WIPE fillets, steaks or whole fish with paper towels. Or, rinse them quickly with cold water and pat dry.

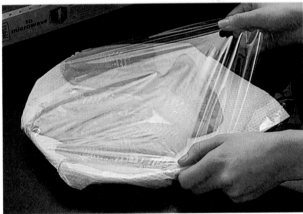

REFRIGERATE fish on paper towels. Cover them tightly with plastic wrap or aluminum foil.

How to Super-Chill Fish

STIR 1 pound of coarse ice cream salt into 20 pounds of crushed ice to make a salt-ice mixture. If less is needed, cut the ingredients accordingly. Line the cooler with 4 inches of crushed ice. Leave the drain open.

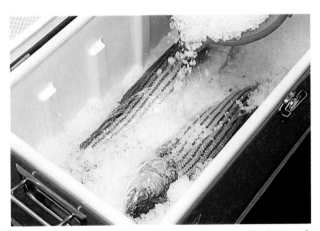

PLACE wrapped fish on the crushed ice. Add a layer of the salt-ice mixture and then more fish. Alternate layers, finishing with a generous topping of salt-ice. Keep the cooler lid tightly closed.

Freezing and Thawing Fish

Freezing is a convenient way to preserve the quality of fish. Freeze them immediately after cleaning unless they will be eaten within 24 hours.

Proper packaging shields the fish from air, which causes freezer burn. Air cannot penetrate ice, so fish frozen in a solid block of ice or with a glaze are well-protected. A double wrap of aluminum foil or plastic wrap and freezer paper is added insurance against air penetration.

Cut fillets into serving-size pieces before freezing. Fish that are being frozen in a block of ice often float to the top before the water freezes. If this happens, add a little ice water and freeze again before double-wrapping. Glazed fish should be checked periodically and the glaze renewed, if necessary.

Store fish in a 0° freezer. If ice cream remains firm, the freezer should be adequate. A frost-free freezer is not recommended, because the fan pulls moisture

How to Freeze Fish in a Block of Ice

SELECT plastic containers, thoroughly washed milk cartons, or small cake or bread pans to freeze whole fish, fillets or steaks.

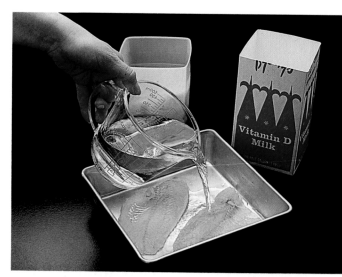

PACK fish for one meal in a container, leaving 1½ inches of airspace; or, layer fish on bottom of pan. Cover fish with very cold water. Freeze the fish in the pan.

Alternate Freezing Techniques

DOUBLE-WRAP whole fish, steaks or fillets that are frozen without a protective block of ice. Separate the fillets or steaks with waxed paper to make thawing easier. This method saves freezer space.

GLAZE whole fish by first freezing without wrapping. Dip frozen fish in very cold water; freeze again. Repeat three to five times, until ⅛ inch of ice builds up. Double-wrap in airtight package, handling fish carefully.

from wrapped fish and quickly causes freezer burn. The chart (right) shows storage times. For top quality, cook within the suggested time.

Fish fillets and steaks may be treated to extend their freezer life by 3 months. Mix 2 tablespoons of ascorbic acid (available in drugstores) and 1 quart water. Place fish in the mixture for 20 seconds. Double-wrap and freeze immediately.

Never thaw fish at room temperature. Bacteria flourishes in warm temperatures. Use the thawing methods described below.

Freezer Storage Chart

TYPE	WHOLE	STEAKS	FILLETS
Large Oily	2 months	1½ months	1 month
Small Oily	1½ months	1 month	1 month
Large Lean	6 months	4 months	3½ months
Small Lean	4 months	3 months	2½ months

COVER milk carton with aluminum foil. Place lid on plastic container. Freeze. Pop out block of frozen fish from the pan by running cold water on the bottom.

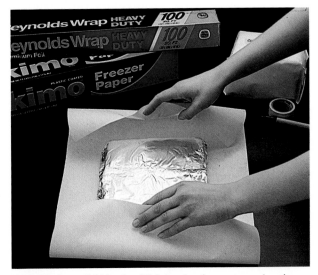

WRAP the solid block of fish in plastic wrap or aluminum foil. Overwrap with freezer paper, sealing tightly. Label package; include species, date and number of servings.

How to Thaw Fish

MELT the block of ice under cold, running water. When fish are free from ice, place them on a plate lined with paper towels. Cover the fish with plastic wrap and thaw in the refrigerator.

THAW ice-free fish by refrigerating them for 24 hours. To speed the process, place the fish in a heavy, *waterproof* plastic bag. Seal the bag, put it in a bowl of cold water and refrigerate. Or, thaw the fish in a microwave (page 59).

Cooking Techniques

Fish Substitution Guide

All of the gamefish listed in this book's recipes can be replaced by other fish. But for best results, use a fish from the same grouping on the Fish Substitution Chart (below). For example, northern pike, walleye or muskellunge can be substituted in a recipe that calls for largemouth bass.

Fish Substitution Chart

TYPE	SPECIES NAME	OTHER COMMON NAMES
Large Oily (2 pounds and larger)	Salmon:	
	Chinook	King salmon, tyee
	Coho	Silver salmon
	Sockeye	Red salmon
	Pink	Humpback
	Chum	Dog salmon
	Atlantic	Land-locked salmon, Sebago salmon
	Trout:	
	Brook	Squaretail, speckled trout
	Brown	Loch Leven trout, German brown
	Rainbow	Steelhead, Kamloops
	Cutthroat	Yellowstone trout
	Lake	Gray trout, togue, Mackinaw
Small Oily (up to 2 pounds)	Salmon:	
	Kokanee	Sockeye, red salmon
	Trout:	
	Brook	Squaretail, speckled trout
	Brown	Loch Leven trout, German brown
	Rainbow	Steelhead, Kamloops
	Cutthroat	Yellowstone trout
Large Lean (2 pounds and larger)	Black Bass:	
	Largemouth	Black bass
	Smallmouth	Bronzeback, black bass
	Muskellunge	Muskie
	Northern Pike	Jack, pickerel, snake
	Striped Bass	Rockfish, stripers
	Walleye	Walleyed pike, pickerel, doré
	White Bass	Stripers, silver bass
Small Lean (up to 2 pounds)	Panfish:	
	Bluegill	Bream, sunfish
	Yellow perch	Ringed perch, striped perch
	Crappie	Papermouth, speckled perch
	Pumpkinseed	Bream, sunfish
	Black Bass:	
	Largemouth	Black bass
	Smallmouth	Bronzeback, black bass
	White Bass	Stripers, silver bass
Catfish and Bullheads	Catfish:	
	Flathead	Yellow cat, mud cat
	Channel	Fiddler
	Blue	White cat, silver cat
	Bullhead	Horned pout

Recommended Cooking Methods

Cooking methods differ for oily and lean gamefish. Oily fish are best cooked with little or no added oil. They can be broiled, baked, poached, steamed, grilled or smoked. These cooking methods allow the oil to drain from the fish before serving. Small stream trout, however, are often panfried, because they have less fat content than large oily fish such as coho and chinook salmon.

Baste lean fish to keep them moist. They can be panfried, deep-fried, oven fried, baked, broiled, steamed, poached, grilled or smoked.

A common rule of thumb is that white-fleshed fish is lean; dark or pink flesh is oily. Although fish usually have a delicate or mild flavor, oily fish sometimes are strong-tasting. To reduce the oily taste, choose a recipe using lemon or lime juice, wine or vinegar.

Lean fish have fewer calories than oily ones. However, vegetable oil, butter, margarine and sauces add extra calories. Poaching and steaming are the only cooking methods in which no calories are added. Below is a guide to the average number of calories per 4-ounce serving of uncooked fish.

Calorie Chart

TYPE	SPECIES NAME	AVERAGE CALORIES (4-ounce serving)
Oily Fish:	Salmon	223 to 254
	Trout (small)	115
	Trout (large)	223
Lean Fish:	Black Bass	119
	Muskellunge	125
	Northern Pike	101
	Striped Bass	120
	Walleye	106
	Panfish	104
	White Bass	112
Catfish		118
Bullhead		96

Cooking Methods Chart

Legend: ▇ Excellent   ▢ Good

		Panfry	Deep-Fry	Broil	Poach	Bake	Oven Fry	Microwave	Barbecue	Smoke-Cook	Open Fire	Fish Boil
Large Oily:	Salmon			▇				▢	▢	▢		▢
	Trout			▢		▢						
Small Oily:	Salmon			▇				▢	▢	▢		
	Trout			▢								
Large Lean:	Black Bass					▢						
	Muskellunge											
	Northern Pike											
	Striped Bass											
	Walleye	▢										
Small Lean:	Panfish	▇										
	Black Bass	▇										
	White Bass	▇		▇								
Catfish												
Bullhead												

Panfrying Fish

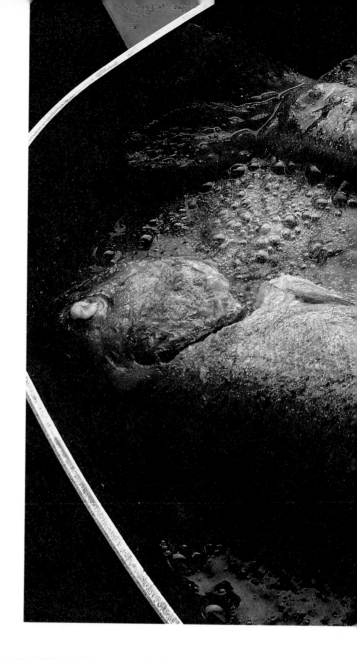

Trout, bluegills, perch and other small fish are excellent when panfried whole. Fillet fish larger than 1½ inches thick. Lean fish are excellent panfried, because oil in the skillet keeps the fish moist. Oily fish are better broiled, grilled, poached or steamed because the natural fat drains away. Small stream trout have less fat and fewer calories than large ones and are very good panfried.

Use a large, heavy skillet to distribute the heat evenly. With most skillets, use ⅛ to ¼ inch of vegetable oil; non-stick skillets require less oil. Add oil as necessary between batches of fish.

Remove the head before cooking. Remove the tail, if desired. Small trout, however, are usually fried with the head and tail left on.

Panfry over medium heat in an uncovered skillet. Do not crowd fish in the skillet. This cools the vegetable oil and makes the fish soggy. Cooking time will range from 5 to 10 minutes, depending on the thickness of the fish. Fish skin should be crisp and brown. The flesh should be moist and flaky.

Drain cooked fish on paper towels. Serve immediately or keep warm in 175° oven while frying more fish.

How to Panfry Whole Fish

COAT the bottom of a heavy skillet with ⅛ to ¼ inch of vegetable oil. Place the skillet over medium heat.

TEST the vegetable oil with a drop of water. It will sizzle when the oil is hot enough for frying.

WIPE the fish with paper towels to remove any moisture, fish slime or loose scales.

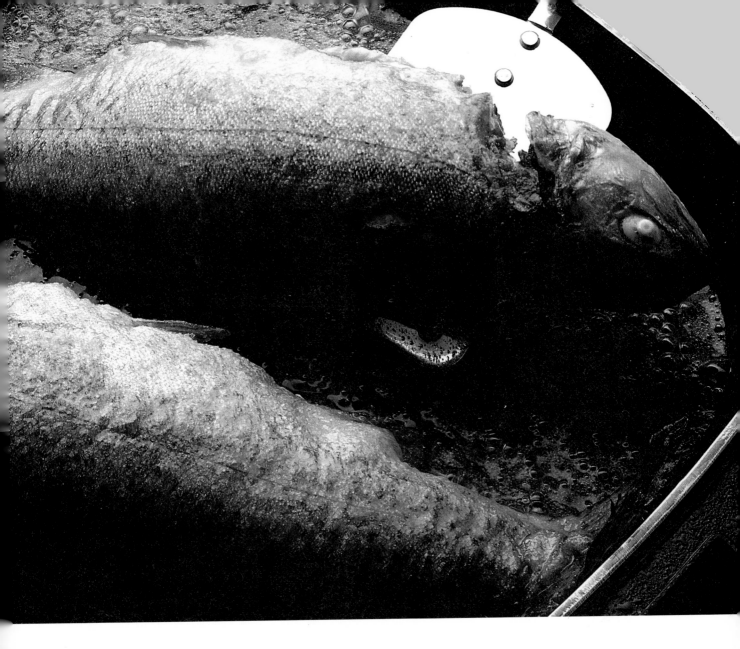

DUST the fish with seasoned flour. Use 1 cup flour, 1 teaspoon salt and ¼ teaspoon pepper.

FRY over medium heat for 3 to 5 minutes on the first side, depending on thickness. Turn; fry 2 to 5 minutes.

INSERT a fork at the backbone and twist. If the fish is done, the flesh will separate easily from the bone.

How to Panfry Fillets

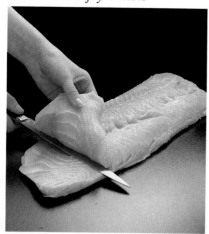

CHOOSE fillets of equal thickness. Fillets over 1½ inches thick should be sliced into thinner fillets.

CUT fillets into serving-size pieces. Dry with paper towels. Heat ⅛ inch of oil in a heavy skillet over medium heat.

COAT the fillets with seasoned flour or a crumb coating (right). Place a few pieces at a time in the skillet.

FRY the first side over medium heat for 3 to 5 minutes, depending on thickness; see chart for cooking times.

TURN and fry the second side. Test for doneness. Flesh is cooked when it flakes easily at the thickest part.

DRAIN on paper towels. Keep fish warm in a 175° oven while frying more fillets. Add oil to the skillet, if needed.

Panfrying Chart

TYPE	SIZE	COOKING TIME 1st Side	COOKING TIME 2nd Side
Whole	up to 1½ inches thick	3 to 5 minutes	2 to 5 minutes
Fillets	¼ inch thick	3 minutes	1 to 2 minutes
	½ inch thick	3 minutes	1½ to 3 minutes
	¾ inch thick	5 minutes	1½ to 3½ minutes
	1 inch thick	5 minutes	2 to 4 minutes

How to Coat With Crumbs

DIP chilled fish in cold milk, cold buttermilk, or a mixture of one beaten egg and 1 to 2 tablespoons cold milk or water. Egg helps to make the coating stick.

COAT dipped fish with flour, pancake mix, Potato Buds®, biscuit mix, cornmeal, or fine bread, cracker or cornflake crumbs.

How to Tell if Fish is Done

UNDERDONE fish is transparent and watery. The flesh does not flake easily with a fork.

JUST-RIGHT fish is opaque and moist. The layers flake easily when tested with a fork.

OVERDONE fish is dry and hard when tested with a fork. The flesh has little taste.

How to Panfry Catfish and Bullheads

PANFRY whole catfish or bullheads only if they are small. Large fish should be filleted before frying. Arrange fish in skillet with thickest portions to center.

TEST for doneness with a fork. Whole fish are done when the flesh easily pulls away from the backbone. The fork should easily penetrate and flake the flesh of fillets.

Deep-Frying Fish

The trick in deep-frying is to form a tasty golden crust to seal out fat. Deep-fried fish tastes best when served quickly. The crust may become soggy if serving is delayed.

One secret to successful deep-frying is proper oil temperature; 375° is recommended. This is the point where vegetable oil bubbles if a small amount of batter is dropped in it. A thermometer is an important piece of equipment. Other necessary tools and utensils are shown below.

Lean fish deep-fry better than oily fish. Fillets, strips or chunks cook most evenly when they are cut to a uniform size.

A layer of newspapers or paper towels under the fryer and the batter bowl makes cleaning up easier.

Vegetable oil may be reused two or three times. After each use, strain through a double thickness of cheesecloth to remove food particles. Store oil in the refrigerator. Add a little fresh oil with each use. Throw away oil when it darkens, or starts to smell and smoke. Pet owners put old oil on dogfood. One tablespoon a day keeps a dog's coat shiny.

Tips for Deep-Frying

EQUIPMENT includes a deep-fryer, mini-fryer, electric frying pan or deep skillet. Other useful tools are a thermometer, wire basket, tongs and a slotted spoon.

VEGETABLE OILS for deep-frying must have a high burning point. Corn, peanut, cottonseed or safflower are popular because they do not change the flavor of the fish.

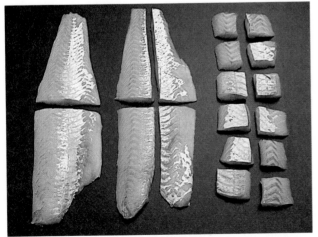

FILLETS must be of a uniform size and shape to deep-fry evenly. Pieces should not be thicker than 1½ inches. They can be left whole or cut into strips or chunks.

WHOLE FISH can be deep-fried if they are less than 1½ inches thick. Deep-fry whole bullheads if they are less than 8 inches long; fillet bigger fish.

Deep-Frying Techniques

There are two ways to deep-fry fish. The most common method requires at least 2 to 3 inches of oil in a traditional deep-fryer or tall saucepan. This is the easiest way, because the deep container controls grease splatters. Fish can also be deep-fried in a large skillet or electric frying pan. Use about 1½ inches of oil and turn the fish during cooking.

Before deep-frying, test-fry one piece of fish. If the batter is too thin and falls off fish, add more flour to the mixture. If the batter is too thick, add a few drops of liquid. Dredging fish in flour or cornstarch before dipping helps the batter stick to the fish.

How to Deep-Fry Fish

CHILL fish in the refrigerator before deep-frying. Pat dry with paper towels. Pour 2 to 3 inches of oil into the deep-fat fryer. Heat to 375°.

DIP a piece of fish in cold batter with fingers, fork or tongs. Use paper towels or newspapers under the bowl and fryer to catch any splatters.

How to Deep-Fry in a Skillet

POUR 1 to 1½ inches of oil into a deep skillet or electric frying pan. Heat oil to 375°. Gently add batter-covered fish, using tongs or your fingers.

FRY fish 2 to 3 minutes, depending on thickness. See chart (right). Turn with spatula and fork to avoid splatters. Fry 1 to 2 minutes more until golden brown.

Cornstarch also makes the coating crisper. A thorough coating ensures the best cooking.

When deep-frying several batches of fish, allow the oil temperature to return to 375° each time fish are added. Add oil as needed between batches. If the fish and batter are cold and the oil is hot, the coating will seal immediately. The cooked fish will be moist and flaky inside, crisp and golden brown outside.

Deep-Frying Chart

TYPE	SIZE	COOKING TIME
Whole	up to 1½ inches thick	3 to 5 minutes
Fillets	¼ to ½ inch thick	3 to 4 minutes
Chunks or Strips	Times will be shorter; check often.	

DROP the fish gently into the hot oil, one at a time. Do not crowd fish or the oil will cool. Fry until the fish is golden brown. See chart (above) for times.

DRAIN fish on a plate lined with paper towels. Keep them warm in 175° oven if frying more. Add more oil to the fryer, if necessary.

Flour Coating

1 egg
1 tablespoon milk or water
1 cup all-purpose flour
1 teaspoon salt
⅛ teaspoon pepper

Blend egg and milk. Mix flour, salt and pepper. Dip fish in egg mixture, then in flour mixture. Deep-fry as directed.

Packaged Coatings

Popular packaged coatings for deep-frying include corn flour, cracker meal, seasoned coating mix, tempura and other batter mixes. Prepare mixes as directed on package. For variety, substitute beer for liquid in package directions.

Beer Batter

1 cup all-purpose flour
3 tablespoons cornstarch
1 teaspoon salt
½ teaspoon paprika
   Dash nutmeg, optional
1 cup beer
1 tablespoon vegetable oil

1½ cups batter

In medium bowl, mix dry ingredients. Blend in beer and vegetable oil until smooth. Dip fish into batter. Deep-fry as directed.

Broiling Fish

Broiled fish has a pleasing flavor, but the high heat dries fish faster than other cooking methods. There are many ways to reduce this dryness.

Select naturally oily fish. Trout, salmon and lake trout are excellent, because they are basted by their own fat which drips through the rack into the broiler pan during cooking.

Baste lean fish often with butter, margarine or vegetable oil to prevent them from drying out. Watch them carefully so they do not overcook.

Lean fish fillets or steaks can be marinated for a few minutes before broiling in a mixture of ½ cup melted butter and 1 tablespoon lemon juice. Use the same mixture for basting. Oily fish can be basted to enhance flavor.

Professional chefs have a secret for serving moist broiled fish. They poach or steam the fish until it is almost cooked. Then, they baste the fish with butter and brown it quickly under the broiler.

Another tip for adding moisture is to pour ¼ to ½ inch of boiling liquid, such as a fish stock, wine, beer

or vegetable juice, into the broiler pan. Place the fish on the oiled rack and cook as directed. The fish will be bathed with hot steam while it is browning.

When cooking fillets with skin, place skin side up first. Small whole stream trout can be broiled with or without the head. Most fish are placed 4 inches from the heat. Thin fillets are set 5 inches from the heat to keep them from drying out.

Many cooks line the broiler pan and rack with aluminum foil for easy cleanup. Poke holes in the foil so the oil drains into the pan, avoiding flare-ups.

If using an electric range, broil with the door slightly ajar. This keeps the heat constant since the broiling unit is always on. Close the door if using a gas range.

Broiling Chart

TYPE/ SIZE	COOKING TIME 1st Side	COOKING TIME 2nd Side	DISTANCE FROM HEAT
Whole up to 2 inches thick	5 min.	4 to 8 min.	4 inches
Fillets			
¼ inch	3 to 4 min.	—	5 inches
½ inch	3 min.	1 to 3 min.	4 inches
¾ inch	3 min.	2½ to 3¼ min.	4 inches
Steaks			
1 inch	5 min.	2 to 4 min.	4 inches

How to Broil Whole Fish

SELECT a whole fish that is about 10 to 14 inches long. It should be no thicker than 2 inches. Pat the fish dry with paper towels.

BRUSH the broiler pan with vegetable oil. Adjust the pan, so it is 4 inches from heat. Set oven to broil and/or 550°. Place the fish on the broiler pan.

BASTE the fish with vegetable oil, melted margarine or butter. Broil for 5 minutes on the first side; baste once during cooking.

TURN the fish carefully with a spatula or tongs. Try to avoid piercing the skin. Baste again. Broil for 4 to 8 minutes; baste once more during cooking.

TEST for doneness by pulling the dorsal fin. If it is easily removed, the fish is cooked. Insert a fork next to the backbone. The flesh should flake easily.

SAVE the juice from the broiler pan to use in sauces or chowder. Drain the fish on paper towels and serve on a heated plate. See page 74 for serving tips.

How to Broil Fillets

CUT the fillets into serving-size pieces. Brush the broiler pan with oil. Adjust the pan, so it is 4 inches from heat. Set oven to broil and/or 550°. Place fillets on the pan.

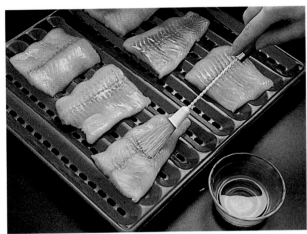

BASTE the fillets with oil, margarine or butter. If the fillets have skin, start them with the skin side up. Broil on the first side. See chart (page 45) for cooking times.

TURN and broil on the second side, basting again. Test for doneness with a fork. The fish is done when the flesh flakes easily at the thickest part.

THIN FILLETS of ¼ inch are arranged on an oiled broiler pan 5 inches from heat. Broil as directed for other fillets, but do not turn over. See chart (page 45) for times.

How to Broil Steaks

BRUSH the broiler pan with oil. Adjust the pan, so it is 4 inches from heat. Set oven to broil and/or 550°. Place steaks on the pan; baste. Broil on first side for 5 minutes.

TURN the steaks over; broil on the second side for 2 to 4 minutes, depending on the thickness. Baste again. Steaks are done when the flesh flakes easily.

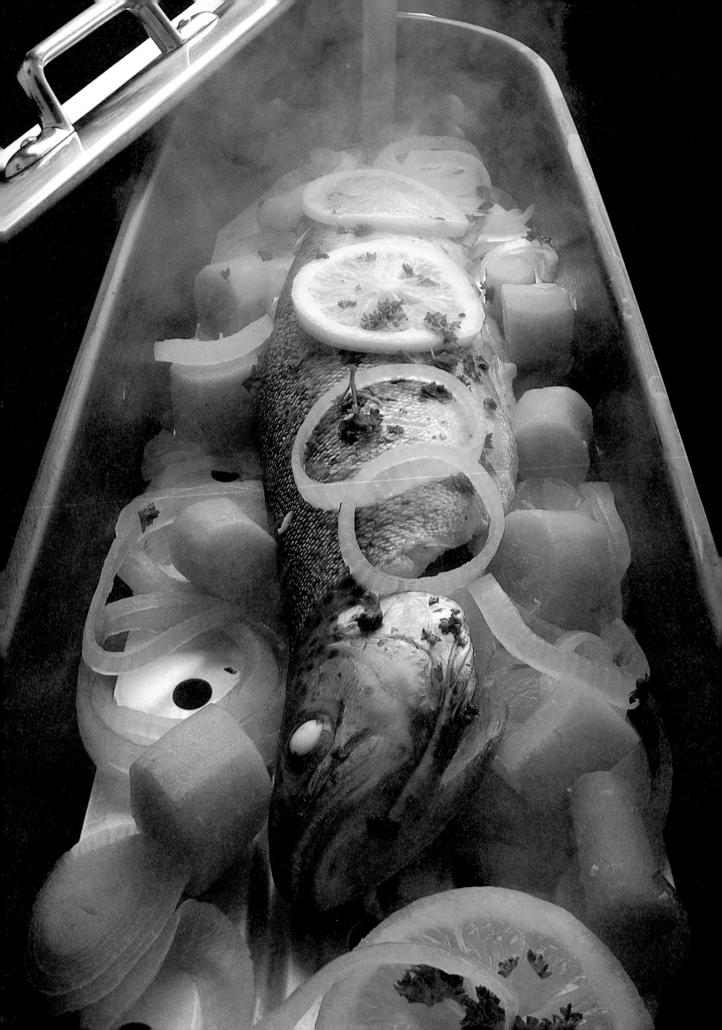

Poaching & Steaming Fish

Poaching and steaming enhance the natural taste of all gamefish. Firm-fleshed, oily fish such as salmon and large trout are especially suitable for these easy methods. The oil drains out of the fish into the cooking liquid.

Steaks, fillets or whole fish can be cooked by either method. Fish poachers are usually no longer than 24 inches. Remove the head if the fish is too long for the poacher. However, the head should be cooked in the poaching liquid, because its flesh is especially flavorful. If the fish is still too large to fit into the poacher, cut it into fillets or steaks.

Poached or steamed fish is usually served with melted butter or a sauce. Dieters, who like the low calorie count of fish cooked by these methods, add only a squirt of lemon juice.

Tips for Poaching and Steaming

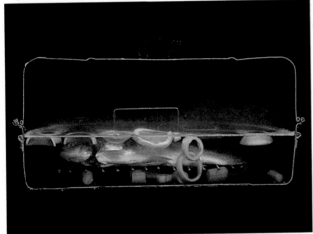

POACHING is cooking fish covered with a simmering vegetable broth or court bouillon (page 50).

STEAMING is cooking fish on a rack above a boiling liquid, usually water and wine. The fish is not immersed.

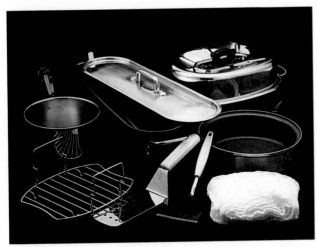

POACHING EQUIPMENT includes fish poachers, long roasting pans, deep skillets or saucepans. A rack with handles, cheesecloth, or large spatulas are useful for removing the fish from the liquid.

STEAMING EQUIPMENT includes steamers, electric frying pans, woks, skillets and saucepans. A rack is necessary to keep the fish above the bubbling liquid. Cheesecloth can also be used to suspend the fish.

Poaching and Steaming Techniques

Cooking times are not as critical for poaching and steaming as they are for other methods. Fish cooked a few minutes too long will not be overdone. Cooking time is 9 to 11 minutes per inch thickness, measured at the thickest part, unless the fish is partially frozen. Then the time must be slightly increased.

Leave the skin on fillets to keep the flesh intact. The skin can be removed before serving, if desired.

Serve the fish either hot or cold. Remove the skin from whole fish and garnish before serving. See page 74 for serving tips. Serve with lemon juice, a lemon-butter mixture or a favorite sauce. When cooking a whole fish, allow ½ to ¾ pound per serving. Leftovers can be used in salads, chowders or fish cakes.

After the fish is cooked, the liquid can be reduced by half over high heat and saved for use in soups or chowders. Store in 1- or 2-cup plastic containers in the freezer. Instructions for thawing in the microwave are on page 59.

Court Bouillon

8 cups water*
1 large carrot, cut into 1-inch pieces
1 medium onion, sliced or chopped
2 or 3 lemon slices
1 tablespoon snipped fresh parsley
⅛ teaspoon peppercorns
1 bay leaf

Combine all ingredients in a fish poacher; cover. Prepare as directed (right).

*Substitute 6½ cups water plus 1½ cups white wine.

Poaching and Steaming Chart

TYPE	SIZE	COOKING TIME
Whole	any size	9 to 11 minutes per inch
Fillets	½ inch thick	4 to 6 minutes
	¾ inch thick	6 to 8 minutes
	1 inch thick	9 to 11 minutes
Steaks	¾ inch thick	6 to 8 minutes
	1 inch thick	9 to 11 minutes

How to Steam Fish

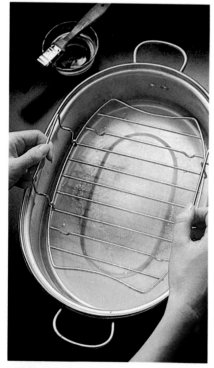

BOIL 1 inch of water or a combination of 10 parts water to 1 part white wine in the steamer. Grease rack with oil. Place in pan over the liquid.

PLACE whole fish, fillets or steaks on the rack. Allow enough space between the fish for steam to circulate. Cover the pan.

STEAM over the boiling liquid. See chart (above) for times. Cook until fish flakes easily at thickest part. See page 74 for serving tips.

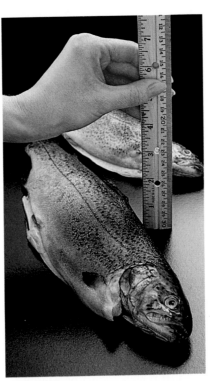

PREPARE ingredients for court bouillon as directed at left. Place poacher on stove, covering two burners, if necessary. Heat to boiling. Reduce heat; cover. Simmer 15 minutes.

MEASURE a whole fish at the thickest point to determine the cooking time. Estimate total cooking time at 9 to 11 minutes per inch thickness. Wipe fish inside and out with paper towels.

PLACE fish on rack; lower into the simmering liquid. If cooking fish without a rack, wrap it in a long piece of cheesecloth. Use the ends as handles to lift the fish.

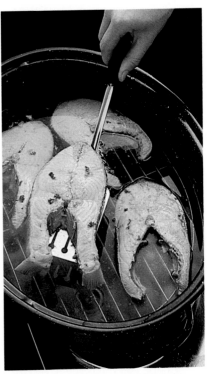

ADD boiling water, if necessary, to cover the fish. Cover poacher and quickly return liquid to boiling. Reduce heat. Simmer for estimated time.

TEST for doneness by inserting a fork at the backbone between the dorsal fin and the head. Twist tines. The fish is done when it flakes easily.

STEAKS AND FILLETS are poached, using the same technique, until they flake easily. See chart for times. Remove with a large spatula.

51

Baking Fish

Baking is ideal for stuffed whole fish and for thick cuts which might dry out under direct heat. Fillets and steaks can also be baked.

Basting with pan juices helps prevent dryness. To brown a dish of baked fillets or steaks before serving, baste with pan juices and place them under a hot broiler for about a minute.

Leave the head on a whole fish if there is room in the pan. Whole fish can be baked with a rice, vegetable or bread stuffing.

A large whole fish is difficult to remove from the pan. If desired, place the fish on greased aluminum foil before putting it in the pan. Pick up the foil to remove the fish. Large spatulas are also helpful.

Utensils for baking whole fish include long roasting pans or casseroles. Use a rack to keep oily fish out of the cooking juices. Bake fillets and steaks in a shallow 8×8- or 13×9-inch baking pan.

Baking Chart

TYPE	COOKING TIME
Whole	10 min. plus 9 to 12 min./lb.
Fillets	10 min. plus 10 to 15 min./lb.
Steaks	10 min. plus 10 to 15 min./lb.

WIPE fillets, steaks or a whole fish with paper towels. Heat oven to 375°. Oil a baking pan or rack. Place the fish in the pan. Brush with a mixture of 1 tablespoon lemon juice and ½ cup melted butter.

COVER the baking pan with a lid or aluminum foil and place it in the hot oven. Bake, basting with the lemon-butter mixture two times during cooking. See chart (page 53) for cooking times.

TEST fish for doneness by inserting a fork at the thickest part. In whole fish, test at the backbone between the head and the dorsal fin. Twist the tines. The fish is done when it flakes easily.

REMOVE the fish carefully from the pan. Place it on a heated serving platter. Save the pan juices for use in chowder or sauces. See page 74 for removing the skin and for other serving tips.

Oven Frying Fish

The advantage with oven frying is that it crisps and browns the fish without much cooking oil. It also reduces frying odors.

As with panfrying, lean fish oven fry better than oily ones. For best results, use fillets; whole fish and steaks are less suitable for this method. Choose a baking pan that is large enough so the fillets fit in a single layer without crowding.

Oven Frying Chart

TYPE	SIZE	COOKING TIME
Fillets	¼ inch	9 to 10 minutes
	½ inch	10 to 11 minutes
	¾ inch	11 to 12 minutes

How to Oven Fry Fillets

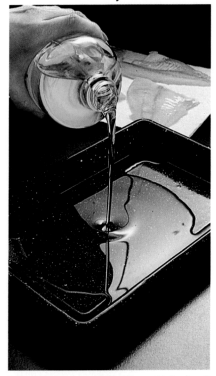

HEAT oven to 450°. Place ⅛ inch of vegetable oil in baking pan. Heat the pan in the oven for 5 minutes. Wipe fillets with paper towels.

BEAT one egg and 1 tablespoon milk in shallow bowl. Spread ½ cup dry seasoned bread crumbs on a plate. Dip fillets in egg, then coat in crumbs.

PLACE the fillets in the hot pan, turning to coat both sides with oil. Oven fry until flesh flakes easily with a fork; see chart (above) for times.

Microwaving Fish

Timing is critical when microwaving fish because they can be easily overcooked. Ideally, the fish should be removed from the oven *just* before it flakes. Watch carefully as it cooks.

Lean fish is usually microwaved at 100% power. Oily fish is microwaved at 50% power because the fatty flesh may "pop" at a higher setting.

When cooked and flaked fish is needed for a recipe, microwave using the basic technique (below) or by the steaming technique (page 58).

Poaching Ingredients

¼ cup water
1 medium carrot, cut into ½-inch pieces
1 stalk celery, cut into 1-inch pieces
1 small onion, sliced
3 slices lemon
⅛ teaspoon whole peppercorns
1 bay leaf
1 teaspoon dried parsley flakes
¼ teaspoon salt

Microwaving Chart

TYPE	SIZE	POWER LEVEL	BASIC MICRO-WAVING TIME	POACHING TIME	STEAMING TIME
Small Whole Fish	1 to 1¾ inch	50%	8 to 11 min./lb.	6½ to 10 min./lb.	6½ to 9½ min./lb.
Lean Fillets	½ to 1 inch	100%	2 to 5 min./lb.	3½ to 6½ min./lb.	2½ to 4½ min./lb.
Oily Fillets	½ to 1 inch	50%	5 to 8 min./lb.	5½ to 8½ min./lb.	5 to 7 min./lb.
Lean Steaks	about 1 inch	100%	5 to 8 min./lb.	7 to 9 min./lb.	4½ to 7 min./lb.
Oily Steaks	about 1 inch	50%	8½ to 11½ min./lb.	9½ to 12 min./lb.	7½ to 9½ min./lb.

How to Microwave Fish

BRUSH fish with melted butter or lemon juice. Roll in crumbs, if desired. Place on the roasting rack.

COVER with waxed paper (except crumb-coated fish which gets soggy). Microwave half the time; see chart.

REARRANGE fish, placing less cooked parts to the outside. Microwave remaining time, until fish flakes.

How to Poach Fish in the Microwave

PLACE poaching ingredients (page 57) in a 12 × 8-inch glass baking dish. Cover with plastic wrap and microwave at 100% power until water is bubbling, 4 to 6 minutes.

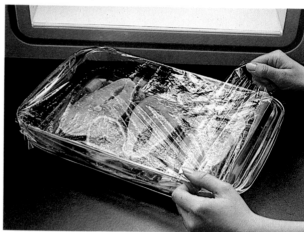

PUT fish in dish. Cover tightly with plastic wrap, turning one edge back to allow steam to escape. Microwave for half the time; see chart (page 57) for times.

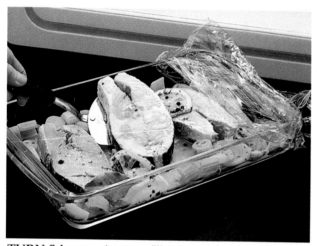

TURN fish over. Arrange fillets so thick parts are to the outside and thin parts overlap. Cover with vented plastic wrap and microwave remaining time.

REMOVE fish from the oven. Test for doneness by probing the thickest part with a fork. Serve immediately. See page 74 for serving tips.

How to Steam Fish in the Microwave

PLACE fish on the microwave roasting rack. Thickest portions should be to the outside.

COVER the baking dish tightly with plastic wrap. Turn back one edge to allow steam to escape.

MICROWAVE for half the time; see chart (page 57) for times. Rotate dish; microwave until fish flakes easily.

Thawing Fish in the Microwave

Thawing fish in the microwave is easy if the fish are rearranged so the less thawed parts are toward the outside of the roasting rack. Separate frozen serving-size pieces before thawing. If this cannot be done, break them apart as soon as possible.

Glazed fish and those frozen without ice can be thawed in the microwave. A block of ice must be removed before microwave thawing, because fish can partially cook before the ice melts. Wipe ice off glazed fish as it thaws and remove water that accumulates in the roasting rack.

Remove the fish when it is pliable but still a bit icy in the thick parts. Thawing continues during the stand-ing time. Drain and cook immediately, or cover and refrigerate until mealtime.

Flaked fish can be easily thawed. Place the un-wrapped fish in a small dish. Microwave 1 cup of fish at 50% power for 2 to 3 minutes; 2 cups for 2½ to 4½ minutes, until the fish is thawed, but still cold. Use a fork to break up the chunks after half the microwaving time. Let it stand 5 minutes and drain.

To thaw fish stock, place it in a small bowl. Micro-wave 1 cup of the stock at 100% power for 2 to 3 minutes; 2 cups for 3 to 4½ minutes, until it is thawed, but still cool. Use a fork to break up the stock. Let it stand for 5 minutes.

Thawing Chart

TYPE	SIZE	POWER LEVEL	FROZEN WITHOUT ICE	GLAZED
Small Whole	1 to 1¾ inches thick	50%	3½ to 6½ min./lb.	4 to 6½ min./lb.
Fillets	¼ to 1 inch thick	50%	3 to 5 min./lb.	3½ to 5½ min./lb.
Steaks	about 1 inch thick	50%	3 to 5½ min./lb.	3½ to 6 min./lb.

How to Thaw Fish

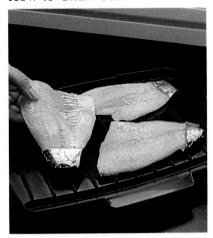

PLACE fish on microwave roasting rack. Shield thin ends with foil. Micro-wave for half the time; see chart.

TURN fish over. Rearrange fillets so thick parts are to the outside and thin parts overlap. Remove shields.

MICROWAVE remaining time, until pliable, but still cool. Let stand 5 min-utes to complete thawing.

Barbecuing Fish

Barbecuing fish on the grill is fun and easy with few cleanup chores. Besides, fish always seems to taste better when cooked outdoors.

Pile charcoal briquets in a pyramid shape and light them at least 30 minutes before cooking time. When the briquets turn ashy-grey, they are ready for cooking. Push the briquets into a ring, roughly the shape of the fish. Tossing moist hickory or apple wood chips onto the coals adds a smoky flavor to the fish.

Outdoor cooking time varies considerably, depending upon air temperature, wind, temperature of charcoal, and the distance of the fish from the coals. Test the fish often. Lean fish need to be basted often, because they dry out quickly. Lean fish can be marinated in Italian dressing before cooking; baste with the marinade during cooking.

Equipment for Barbecuing

GRILLS come in all sizes, from a small portable hibachi to a large covered kettle. Some smoke-cookers are also used as charcoal grills.

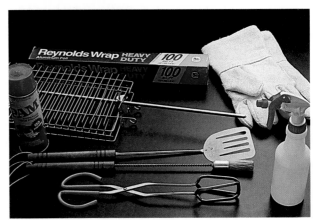

UTENSILS include heavy-duty aluminum foil, a grill basket, flame-retardant gloves, long-handled spatula, tongs and basting brush, a squirt bottle or plant mister to douse flare-ups, and non-stick spray coating.

How to Barbecue Whole Fish

BRUSH the grill with oil, or spray with a non-stick coating. Wipe the fish with paper towels; brush with oil. Spread the coals. Lay fish on the grill. Cover, if desired.

COOK the fish on the first side. See chart (right) for times. Brush with oil or a lemon-butter mixture every 3 to 4 minutes to keep fish from drying.

How to Barbecue Fillets and Steaks

WIPE fish with paper towels. Oil the fish and grill. Place fillets skin side down. Place skinless fillets on foil cut to size. An oiled grill basket is helpful for easy turning.

BASTE fish frequently with oil or a lemon-butter mixture. Cover with a foil tent, if desired. Cook the fish on the first side. See chart (right) for times.

How to Barbecue Fish Wrapped in Foil

SPREAD butter on a large piece of heavy-duty aluminum foil. Wipe the fish with paper towels and place on the foil. Seal the package and place on the hot grill.

COOK for half the time; see chart (right) for times. Turn the package over; turn the foil ends up to avoid losing juices. Cook remaining time, depending on the thickness.

BRUSH the fish with more oil or butter. Turn over carefully without breaking the skin. Cook on the second side. Baste one or two times during cooking.

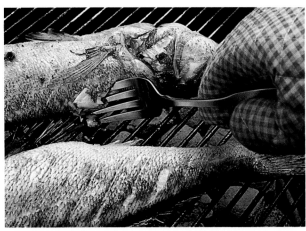

INSERT a fork at the backbone in the thickest part of the fish. Lift the fork; flesh should flake easily. Grill longer, if necessary. Salt and pepper to taste.

TURN fish, except the fillets with skin. Keep the thickest part of the fillet over the hottest coals to insure even cooking. Baste every 2 minutes.

GRILL on second side for 3 to 8 minutes, depending on the thickness. Test by twisting a fork in the flesh. If flesh does not flake, cook a few minutes longer.

Barbecuing Chart

TYPE	SIZE	COOKING TIME 1st Side	COOKING TIME 2nd Side
Whole	up to 2 lbs.	5 min.	3 to 7 min.
	2 to 3 lbs.	10 min.	8 to 12 min.
Fillets	¼ to ¾ inch	3 min.	3 to 8 min.
Steaks	1 inch	5 min.	3 to 8 min.

FISH WRAPPED IN FOIL: Add 1 to 2 minutes to the above times; check often.

UNWRAP the foil carefully. Test the fish with a fork; the flesh should flake easily. If not, rewrap it and grill a few minutes longer.

Smoke-Cooking Fish

Smoked fish is delicious and easy to prepare. Most anglers buy a smoker, though many enjoy making their own. Four items are needed to build a smoker: an enclosure to contain the heat and smoke; a source of heat (often an electric hot plate); wood chips or sawdust to provide smoke; and racks or bars to support the fish. Many books are available with detailed instructions on homemade smokers.

Fish are smoked by two different methods. Smoke-cooking (hot-smoking) is the most popular. It cooks the fish in a few hours, while adding a smoky flavor and a rich color. Smoke-cook fish by following the directions on page 66. The other method, cool-smoking, is more difficult and is not discussed in this book. It is a curing process that requires a larger smokehouse, lower temperature, heavier brine, and up to 2 weeks of time.

Dry-smokers reduce the fish in size and take twice as long as water-smokers. Dry-smoked fish has an intense flavor and is usually served as an appetizer or in salad. It can be refrigerated up to 2 weeks.

Water-smokers (left) have a water pan above the heat source. Fish cooked in a water-smoker are usually served as a main course. The fish is lightly flavored and moist. It can be refrigerated only up to

2 days. Most anglers dry-smoke their fish because they enjoy the concentrated flavor and firm texture.

Commercial smokers (both dry and water) are made with three different heat sources: electric, charcoal and propane. The smoke comes from hardwood sawdust or chips. Hickory, apple, cherry and maple add a delightful flavor. Avoid softwoods and conifers which give fish an unpleasant taste.

Oily fish such as salmon and trout are excellent smoke-cooked. However, all fish are good smoked, so it is fun to experiment. Use whole fish, steaks or fillets. Leave the skin on to keep them intact. Smoking is a good way to use fish that have reached the maximum freezer storage time. After smoking, the fish can be canned or frozen again.

Smoking fish is an inexact process. Cooking time will vary depending on the size of the fish, the air temperature, wind, and the temperature of the heat source. In cold, windy weather, place a commercial dry-smoker in its storage box before smoking. The cardboard adds extra insulation.

Experiment with the brine on the next page. Many cooks try less salt, more sugar, or a little red pepper or tabasco. It is interesting to change the herbs, too. Brining time can also be altered. A short soak will produce a mild-flavored smoked fish; a longer time will strengthen the seasonings. Practice with small amounts of fish until the brining solution and time is just right. You can also experiment with the smoking time. Some people like firm, dry, smoked fish, while others prefer it soft and moist. Adjust the time to suit your taste.

Equipment for Smoke-Cooking

DRY-SMOKERS include electric models, charcoal kettle grills and garbage cans. Sheet metal boxes, wooden barrels, or large cardboard boxes can also be used.

OLD REFRIGERATORS can be converted into dry-smokers. Remove the electric mechanism and drill ventilation holes in the top and bottom.

Brine Solution

1 cup salt
10 cups water
OPTIONAL:
¼ cup granulated or packed
    brown sugar
  Bay leaf
  Chili powder
  Thyme

      Brines 6 to 8 lbs. of fish

Brining Chart

TYPE/SIZE	BRINING TIME
Whole	
up to 4 lbs.	12 to 18 hours
4 lbs. or more	24 to 48 hours
Fillets, Steaks and Chunks	
½ to 1 inch	12 to 18 hours

How to Prepare Fish for Smoke-Cooking

MIX brine solution (left) in a saucepan. Stir and heat until salt and sugar dissolve. Cool brine.

CUT thick fillets, steaks and chunks into 1½- to 2-inch pieces. Place the fish in a *non-metal* container.

How to Smoke-Cook Fish

ARRANGE the fish on oiled racks. Place fillets skin side down. Leave enough space so the smoke will circulate. Add wood chips or sawdust following smoker's directions. A dry-smoker is pictured.

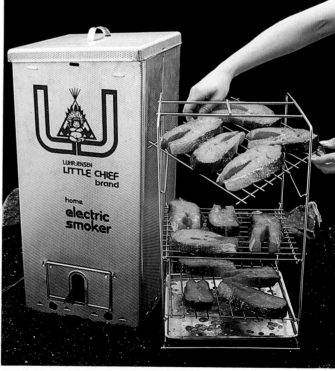

SMOKE the fish following smoker's directions. Dry-smoked fish usually require 6 to 8 hours, using four pans of sawdust. Water-smoked fish average 2 to 3 hours. Rotate racks during smoking for even cooking.

COVER fish with brine and refrigerate; see chart (left). After brining, rinse fish carefully with cold water.

PAT the fish thoroughly dry with paper towels. Place them on a rack over a cookie sheet.

AIR-DRY for 60 minutes until the fish are shiny and dry. Place them in front of a fan to speed drying.

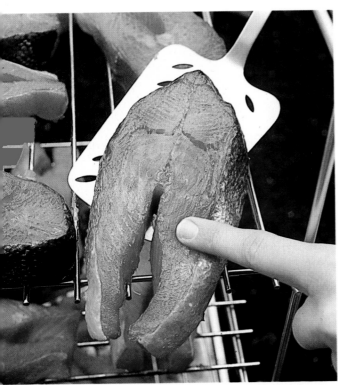

CHECK for doneness. Remove fish from a dry smoker when most of the moisture is gone, but the fish is still soft and flexible. Fish cooked in a water smoker should flake when a fork is twisted in the flesh.

COOL fish thoroughly, and place them in a plastic container or bag. Store in the refrigerator for up to 2 weeks. Freeze (page 30) or can (page 150) a large batch of smoked fish for longer storage.

Open Fire Cooking

Fish cooked over an open fire are delicious. However, they are easily overcooked when the fire is too hot. Keep the fire small and the heat under control. The best woods are maple, birch, apple, hickory, beech and other hardwoods. They burn well and give fish a pleasant flavor. Softwoods such as pine, spruce and hemlock impart an unpleasant taste.

Cook whole fish over an open fire with the head and tail intact to help seal in juices. Keeping the skin on a fillet holds it in one piece and shields it from intense heat. If the skin is removed, protect the fillet with aluminum foil cut to size.

Equipment for open fire cooking includes grates, backyard fireplaces, picnic area fire rings or cement blocks. Useful utensils include heavy-duty aluminum foil, flame retardant gloves, long-handled spatula and tongs, a grill basket, and a cast-iron or heavy aluminum skillet for panfrying.

Tips for Open Fire Cooking

A SMALL FIRE is important. If it is too large, fish will burn on the outside, but will be raw on the inside. Gather an ample supply of dry twigs and add them to the fire at regular intervals to provide even heat.

HOT COALS are best for open fire cooking with a grate. Build a large fire and let it burn down. Start to cook when the flames are out. Spread the glowing coals roughly into the shape of the fish.

STEAM fish by wrapping it securely in greased, heavy-duty aluminum foil. Place the package in hot coals; see chart (page 71) for cooking guidelines. Turn fish one or two times. Check often for doneness.

ROAST small whole fish over an open fire by impaling it on the sharpened end of a sturdy, green, hardwood stick. Cook until flesh at backbone flakes easily. Cool slightly and eat in a corn-on-the-cob fashion.

How to Cook Fish on Grate Over Open Fire

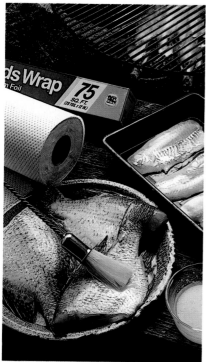

BRUSH the grate and fish with oil, melted margarine or butter. Lean fish need more basting than oily types, such as large trout and salmon.

SPREAD the hot coals. Put the fish on the grate when all flame has died out. Place fillets skin side down, or skinless fillets on foil cut to size.

COOK fish on the first side; see chart (right) for times. Turn; baste with oil, margarine or butter. (Do not turn fillets with skin.) Cook the second side.

How to Panfry Over Open Fire

WIPE fish with paper towels. Panfry whole fish up to 1½ inches thick; fillets and steaks up to 1 inch. Cut thicker fillets into two thinner pieces.

POUR ⅛ inch of oil into a cast-iron or heavy aluminum skillet. Place over small fire or hot coals. Heat until oil sizzles when a drop of water is added.

COAT fish with flour. Season with salt and pepper. Fish can also be fried uncoated. Fry first side; see chart (right) for times.

TEST the fish by probing with a fork; twist the tines. The flesh should flake easily at the thickest part. Cook longer, if necessary.

TENT the fish with a hood of heavy-duty aluminum foil, if you need to protect them from wind, rain or cold. A tent also reflects the heat.

ALTERNATE METHODS include wrapping greased fish in aluminum foil or placing them in a grill basket. Cook over hot coals on the grate.

Open Fire Cooking Chart

METHOD/ TYPE	SIZE	COOKING TIME 1st Side	COOKING TIME 2nd Side
GRATE Whole	up to 2 pounds	8 minutes	8 to 12 minutes
	2 to 3 pounds	10 minutes	10 to 15 minutes
Fillets and Steaks	up to ½ inch	3 minutes	1 to 4 minutes
	½ to 1 inch	5 minutes	3 to 5 minutes
PANFRY Whole	up to 1½ inches	5 minutes	4 to 6 minutes
Fillets and Steaks	¼ to ½ inch	3 minutes	2 to 4 minutes
	½ to 1 inch	5 minutes	1 to 5 minutes

WRAPPED IN FOIL ON GRATE: Add 1 to 2 minutes to the above times; check often.

WRAPPED IN FOIL IN THE COALS: Use the above times as a guide, but the time will be shorter. Check often.

TURN; fry second side. Keep adding twigs to the fire to maintain an even heat. Cook until the flesh flakes easily at the thickest part.

Open Fire Cooking: Great Lakes Fish Boil

Fish boils are popular along the shores of the Great Lakes. Lumbermen originated them over 100 years ago when they wanted easy one-pot meals.

For best results, use large, oily fish such as lake trout, salmon, brown trout and steelhead. Always scale the fish and cut it into steaks. The skin and bones will hold the fish together during cooking. The fish can be fresh or thawed. Use medium-sized potatoes, because they are normally done the same time as the fish.

Special fish boil kettles are usually 8-quart or 12-quart pots. However, any large, sturdy pot with vents in the lid and a basket will work. The ingredients (right) are for an 8-quart kettle. In a 12-quart pot, double the food ingredients, but increase the water just enough to cover the food.

For good results, the water must actively bubble for the entire 30 minutes of cooking time. Maintaining a hard boil requires a large fire and a good supply of dry wood.

How to Prepare a Fish Boil

BUILD a large fire. Enclose it on three sides with cement blocks. Place a sturdy grill rack on the blocks. Have extra wood ready to maintain the fire.

PLACE the kettle on the rack. Remove the basket. Add water (above). Cover, with vents open, and heat the water to boiling.

SCRUB the potatoes, but do not peel. Cut a thin slice from each end. Put the potatoes in the basket. Remove the skin from the onions.

Fish Boil Ingredients

In 8-quart kettle:

5 quarts water
6 medium potatoes
6 onions
1 cup salt
3 pounds fish steaks, 1 to 1½
    inches thick, scaled

6 servings

LOWER the basket into the boiling water; cover. Return to boiling. Add onions and salt; cover. Boil, with vents open, for 18 minutes.

ADD the steaks to the basket. Cover and return to boiling. Boil 12 minutes. Test potatoes and fish with a fork. The fish should flake easily. Remove the basket; drain thoroughly. Serve immediately with lemon wedges and melted butter. Coleslaw and hard rolls are traditional accompaniments.

Serving Tips for Fish

Fish tastes better when it is attractively served. Alone, cooked fish is often white and dull-looking.

Greens such as parsley, watercress and lettuce add color and appeal to a platter of cooked fish. Attractive vegetables such as cherry tomatoes, peas, carrots, broccoli and string beans also dress up a plate. Other pretty and tasty garnishes include olives, carrot curls, green and red peppers, cucumbers, radishes, pimientos, lemons and limes. Colorful plates are also a good idea for serving fish.

Lemons are especially popular as garnish for fish. The lemon juice enhances the flavor without adding calories. Salt-conscious dieters use the juice as a substitute for salt. Limes are a good alternative to lemons, especially when they are reasonably priced.

Fish is often served with a sauce. A light, mild sauce goes well with lean fish. A spicy or tomato sauce complements oily or strong-flavored fish. See page 138 for recipes.

WHOLE FISH. Place on a bed of greens. Peel off the

STEAKS. Serve with attractive vegetables. Use a fork and fingers to peel the skin off in a strip.

skin with a knife and fingers. Replace the eye with a black or green olive and garnish attractively.

FILLETS. Garnish with sprigs of greens, colorful vegetables and fruits.

How to Remove Bones From Cooked Fish

LOOSEN the skin with a knife. Using fingers and knife, carefully peel the skin, starting from behind the head and working across the body to the tail.

INSERT a fork at the backbone. Lift the side carefully away from the spine. On a small fish, the entire side may come off in one piece.

How to Prepare Garnishes

SELECT colorful vegetables to carve into (clockwise from top) cucumber cups, green onion curls, carrot curls, radish roses, cucumber twists or mushroom flowers.

CUT lemons and limes into wedges, slices or twists; or use strips of lemon or lime peel to accompany fish. A squirt of fresh juice is often the only garnish needed.

GRASP the spine behind the head with fingers. Use the fork to hold the fish on the plate. Remove the spine from the fish and discard.

REMOVE fins with the fork and discard. Check both sides of the fish for little rib bones. If any remain, remove them. The fish is now ready to eat.

Wines to Serve With Fish

DRY, WHITE WINES are usually served with fish. However, light red wines may be the best complement for spicy fish recipes.

Wine Chart

RECIPE STYLE	WINE TYPE	GENERAL TASTE
Fried Fish	Columbard	Semi-dry
	Chablis	Semi-dry to dry
	Rosé	Semi-dry
Baked Fish	Chenin Blanc	Semi-dry
	Chardonnay	Semi-dry to dry
	Reisling (Moselle & Rhine)	Moderately sweet
Poached or Steamed Fish	Chardonnay	Semi-dry to dry
	Fume Blanc	Semi-dry
	Soave (Italian)	Semi-dry
Fish with Spicy or Tomato Sauce	California Burgundy (light American red)	Semi-dry
	Bardolino (Italian red)	Semi-dry to dry
	Chianti (American)	Semi-dry to dry
	Beaujolais	Semi-dry

Popular American brand names include Almaden, Gallo, California Cellars, Inglenook, Paul Masson, Fetzer and Sebastiani. Most of these wines are available at reasonable prices and in jug sizes.

Recipes

Appetizers

Serve small helpings of appetizers to stimulate the appetite but not satisfy it. Make appetizers from fresh fish or from cooked leftovers. Store leftover fish in the refrigerator no longer than 2 days before using it in appetizers.

Cook appetizers shortly before serving and keep warm in 175° oven. Keep cold appetizers in the refrigerator until serving time.

Sweet and Sour Fish Nuggets

Vegetable oil
½ pound bass or other lean fish fillets (page 34),
    ¼- to ½-inch thick
1 egg
2 teaspoons water
⅓ cup dry bread crumbs
Sweet and Sour Sauce (page 143)

20 to 25 appetizers

In deep-fat fryer or saucepan, heat oil (2 to 3 inches) to 375°. Cut fish into 1½-inch pieces. In small bowl, blend egg and water. Dip fish into egg mixture, then coat with bread crumbs.

Fry a few at a time, turning occasionally, until deep golden brown, 1½ to 2½ minutes. Drain on paper towels. Keep warm in 175° oven. Prepare sauce as directed. Serve fish nuggets with sauce.

Beer-Poached Chunks

Cocktail Sauce (page 141)
½ pound perch or other panfish fillets (page 34),
   ¼- to ½-inch thick
1 can (12 ounces) beer

20 to 25 appetizers

Prepare Cocktail Sauce as directed. Cut fish into 1½-inch pieces. In 1½-quart saucepan, heat beer to boiling. Stir in half of the fish. Reduce heat to medium. Cook, stirring gently, until fish flakes easily, about 2 minutes. Remove with slotted spoon. Repeat. Serve with Cocktail Sauce.

Lemony Fried Fish Balls →

Basic Tartar Sauce (page 139) or Cocktail
  Sauce (page 141)
2 tablespoons finely chopped onion
1 tablespoon margarine or butter
2 tablespoons all-purpose flour
¼ cup half-and-half
½ teaspoon salt
  Dash pepper
1 egg, slightly beaten
1 cup flaked cooked trout or other oily fish
  (page 34)
1 to 1½ teaspoons grated lemon peel
2 tablespoons all-purpose flour
1 teaspoon water
¼ cup fine dry bread crumbs
  Vegetable oil

18 to 20 appetizers

How to Prepare Lemony Fried Fish Balls

PREPARE one or both sauces as directed. Set aside. In small skillet, cook and stir onion in margarine over medium heat until tender, about 1 minute. Stir in 2 tablespoons flour.

BLEND in half-and-half, salt and pepper. Cook and stir over low heat until mixture is very thick and forms a ball. Remove from heat.

STIR in half (about 2 tablespoons) of the beaten egg. Mix in fish and grated lemon peel. Cover and refrigerate about 30 minutes, until chilled.

82

SPRINKLE 2 tablespoons flour on plate or waxed paper. Drop the chilled fish mixture by scant tablespoonfuls onto flour; roll to coat and shape into balls.

MIX water with remaining half of egg. Pour bread crumbs into small dish. Dip balls in egg mixture; roll in bread crumbs. In deep-fat fryer or saucepan, heat oil (2 to 3 inches) to 375°.

FRY five or six balls at a time, turning occasionally, until deep golden brown, 2½ to 3½ minutes. Drain on paper towels. Keep warm in 175° oven. Serve with sauces.

← Fish Toast

¼ cup all-purpose flour
¼ cup finely chopped almonds
¼ cup water
1 egg
2 tablespoons snipped fresh parsley
1 tablespoon cornstarch
1 teaspoon soy sauce
½ teaspoon salt
½ teaspoon sugar
¼ teaspoon sesame oil
¼ pound walleye or other lean fish fillets
    (page 34), about ½-inch thick
  Vegetable oil
5 slices white bread

20 appetizers

In medium bowl, mix flour, almonds, water, egg, parsley, cornstarch, soy sauce, salt, sugar and oil. Cut fillets into 20 pieces. Stir into flour mixture.

In deep-fat fryer or saucepan, heat vegetable oil (2 to 3 inches) to 375°. Remove crusts from bread; cut each slice into four squares. Top with fish-flour mixture. Fry five squares at a time, turning several times, until golden brown, 2 to 3 minutes. Drain on paper towels. Keep warm in 175° oven.

Salmon Quiche

Crust:
3 cups all-purpose flour
1 teaspoon salt
⅔ cup vegetable oil
¼ cup plus 2 tablespoons milk

Filling:
1 cup shredded Monterey Jack cheese
1 to 1½ cups flaked cooked salmon
5 eggs
2 cups half-and-half
¾ teaspoon salt
⅛ teaspoon pepper
  Dash ground nutmeg
2 tablespoons snipped fresh parsley

36 appetizers

Heat oven to 350°. In medium bowl, mix flour, salt, oil and milk lightly with fork until blended. Pat into 13 × 9-inch baking pan, patting dough 1 inch up side of pan. Bake for 8 minutes.

Sprinkle cheese over hot crust, then sprinkle with fish. In small mixing bowl, blend eggs, half-and-half, salt, pepper and nutmeg. Pour over fish. Sprinkle with parsley. Bake until knife inserted in center comes out clean, 30 to 35 minutes. Cool for 10 minutes. Cut into 2 × 1½-inch pieces.

Broiled Bass Canapés ↑

1 cup flaked cooked bass or other lean fish
  (page 34)
½ cup finely chopped cucumber
2 tablespoons mayonnaise or salad dressing
1 tablespoon dairy sour cream
¼ teaspoon steak sauce
⅛ teaspoon salt
⅛ teaspoon dried dillweed
  Dash pepper
2 drops red pepper sauce
24 to 30 Melba toast rounds or rich round
  crackers
  Sliced pimiento

24 to 30 appetizers

In small bowl, mix fish, cucumber, mayonnaise, sour cream, steak sauce, salt, dillweed, pepper and red pepper sauce. Spread about 1 heaping teaspoonful of mixture on each cracker. Place crackers on baking sheet.

Set oven to broil and/or 550°. Broil 4 inches from heat until light brown, 3 to 5 minutes. Top each with pimiento slice before serving.

Broiled Trout Canapés ↑

1 cup flaked cooked trout or other oily fish
  (page 34)
1 cup shredded Monterey Jack cheese
⅓ cup finely chopped celery
¼ cup dairy sour cream
2 tablespoons finely chopped onion
⅛ teaspoon pepper
30 Melba toast rounds or rich round crackers

30 appetizers

In small bowl, mix fish, cheese, celery, sour cream, onion and pepper. Mound about 1½ teaspoonfuls of mixture on each cracker. Place crackers on baking sheet. Sprinkle with paprika, if desired.

Set oven to broil and/or 550°. Broil 6 inches from heat until cheese melts, 2½ to 3½ minutes.

← Trout Cheese Ball

1 package (3 ounces) cream cheese, softened
¼ cup margarine or butter, softened
1 tablespoon grated onion
1 teaspoon grated lemon peel
½ teaspoon prepared horseradish
¼ teaspoon prepared mustard
⅛ teaspoon salt
⅛ teaspoon pepper
1 cup finely flaked cooked trout or other oily fish
   (page 34)
½ cup finely chopped pecans
3 tablespoons snipped fresh parsley

3½-inch cheese ball

In medium bowl, blend cream cheese, margarine, onion, lemon peel, horseradish, mustard, salt and pepper. Stir in fish. Cover and refrigerate 1 to 2 hours, until chilled.

Mix pecans and parsley; sprinkle on plate or waxed paper. Shape fish mixture into ball. Roll in pecans and parsley to coat. Place on serving plate. Cover and refrigerate 3 to 4 hours. Serve with crackers.

← Salmon Spread

1 package (3 ounces) cream cheese, softened
⅓ cup dairy sour cream
2 tablespoons finely chopped celery
1 tablespoon finely chopped green onion
1 tablespoon fresh lime juice
1½ teaspoons Worcestershire sauce
⅛ teaspoon salt
   Dash pepper
1 cup flaked cooked salmon or other oily fish
   (page 34)

About 1⅓ cups

In small bowl, mix all ingredients except fish. Stir in fish. Cover and refrigerate at least 2 hours. Serve with crackers or bread sticks.

Creamy Dill Dip

1 cup cottage cheese
2 tablespoons mayonnaise or salad dressing
2 tablespoons fresh lemon or lime juice
¼ teaspoon dried dillweed
1 cup finely flaked cooked bass or other lean fish
   (page 34)
2 tablespoons finely chopped almonds

About 2 cups

In food processor or blender, blend cottage cheese, mayonnaise, lemon juice and dillweed until smooth. Stir in remaining ingredients. Cover and refrigerate at least 1 hour. Serve with vegetable dippers.

Smoked Fish Dip ↑

1 cup dairy sour cream
½ cup mayonnaise or salad dressing
1 cup flaked smoked fish
3 tablespoons chopped green onion
½ teaspoon Worcestershire sauce
   Dash garlic powder

About 1½ cups

In small bowl, blend sour cream and mayonnaise. Stir in remaining ingredients. Cover and refrigerate at least 1 hour. Serve with vegetable dippers or potato chips.

Fish Salads

Salads are a good way to use leftover cooked fish. They can also be made from fresh fish. Chill leftover fish in the refrigerator and use for salad within 48 hours. If leftovers are not available, poach, steam or microwave (pages 48 and 56) fresh fish for salad recipes that call for cooked fish. Chill immediately after cooking.

Salmon Potato Salad

⅔ cup dairy sour cream
2 tablespoons plus 1 teaspoon cider vinegar
2 tablespoons chopped green onion
1 tablespoon plus 1 teaspoon sugar
1¼ teaspoons prepared mustard
½ teaspoon salt
    Dash pepper
1 quart water
1 teaspoon salt
2 medium red potatoes (about ¾ pound)
2 cups flaked cooked salmon
1 small onion, finely chopped
¼ cup finely chopped celery
1 tablespoon snipped fresh parsley
4 to 6 tomatoes, optional

4 to 6 servings

In small bowl, blend sour cream, vinegar, green onion, sugar, mustard, ½ teaspoon salt and the pepper. Cover and refrigerate.

In 2-quart saucepan, heat water and 1 teaspoon salt to boiling. Add potatoes. Return to boiling. Reduce heat. Cover and simmer until fork tender, 25 to 35 minutes. Drain. Cool.

Peel potatoes; cut into ½-inch cubes. In medium bowl, combine potatoes, salmon, onion, celery and parsley. Add sour cream dressing, tossing to coat. To serve salad in tomato shells, remove stem ends of tomatoes and scoop out center pulp and seeds.

Confetti Salad

SALAD:
1 medium green pepper
2 cups flaked cooked panfish or other lean fish (page 34)
2 cups shredded carrot
½ cup sliced fresh mushrooms
¼ cup thinly sliced celery
¼ cup sliced black olives
¼ cup snipped fresh parsley
2 radishes, thinly sliced
2 tablespoons chopped onion

DRESSING:
⅓ cup vegetable oil
3 tablespoons cider vinegar
2 teaspoons lemon juice
¼ teaspoon sugar
¼ teaspoon salt
⅛ teaspoon dry mustard
⅛ teaspoon pepper
    Dash garlic powder

4 to 6 servings

Cut green pepper into 2½ × ¼-inch strips. In medium bowl, combine green pepper with remaining salad ingredients.

In small bowl, blend dressing ingredients. Pour over salad, tossing to coat. Refrigerate at least 1 hour. Garnish with lemon slices, if desired.

← Garden Salad

SALAD:

3 cups torn iceberg lettuce
1 cup flaked cooked panfish or other lean fish
   (page 34)
1 large tomato, cut into 8 wedges
2 hard-cooked eggs, sliced
½ small onion, thinly sliced and separated into
   rings, optional
¼ cup sliced green olives
4 radishes, thinly sliced

DRESSING:

¼ cup vegetable oil
3 tablespoons white vinegar
2 tablespoons catsup
⅛ teaspoon pepper

4 to 6 servings

In medium bowl, combine salad ingredients. In small bowl, blend dressing ingredients. Pour dressing over salad, tossing gently to coat.

Trout Salad With Mustard Dressing

DRESSING:

2 packages (3 ounces each) cream cheese,
   softened
⅓ cup mayonnaise or salad dressing
¼ cup half-and-half
1 tablespoon plus 1 teaspoon prepared mustard
⅛ teaspoon celery salt
⅛ teaspoon curry powder
3 to 4 drops red pepper sauce

SALAD:

2 tablespoons margarine or butter, melted
   Dash garlic salt
½ pound raw shrimp, peeled and deveined
1 bunch romaine
3 cups flaked cooked trout
10 cherry tomatoes, quartered
2 hard-cooked eggs, sliced
1 avocado, peeled and sliced
½ cup sliced black olives

4 to 6 servings

In small bowl, blend cream cheese and mayonnaise. Stir in remaining dressing ingredients. Cover and refrigerate dressing at least 1 hour. In small bowl, mix margarine and garlic salt. Set oven to broil and/or 550°. Place shrimp on broiler pan. Brush with margarine. Broil 4 inches from heat until opaque, 4 to 7 minutes, brushing with remaining margarine once. Turn large shrimp over once.

Arrange romaine on large serving plate. Mound fish in center and arrange shrimp and remaining ingredients around fish. Serve with dressing.

Salmon Salad →

   1 cup uncooked small shell macaroni
   2 cups flaked cooked salmon
   ⅓ cup sliced black olives
   ¼ cup finely chopped green pepper
   1 tablespoon grated onion
   ¼ cup vegetable oil
   2 tablespoons red wine vinegar
   ¼ teaspoon dried oregano leaves
   ¼ teaspoon salt
   ⅛ teaspoon pepper

4 to 6 servings

Prepare macaroni as directed on package. Rinse under cold water; drain. In medium bowl, combine macaroni, salmon, olives, green pepper and onion. In small bowl, blend oil, vinegar, oregano, salt and pepper. Pour dressing over salad, tossing to coat. Refrigerate at least 1 hour before serving.

Northern Pike Salad

   2 cups flaked cooked northern pike or other
      lean fish (page 34)
   ⅓ cup mayonnaise or salad dressing
   ¼ cup finely chopped celery
   2 tablespoons finely chopped onion
1½ teaspoons prepared mustard
   ¼ teaspoon salt
   ⅛ teaspoon pepper

4 to 6 servings

In small bowl, blend all ingredients. Refrigerate at least 30 minutes. Serve on lettuce leaves. Sprinkle with paprika, if desired.

Fish Slaw

   3 cups coarsely chopped cabbage
   1 cup flaked cooked bass or other lean fish
      (page 34)
   ¼ cup finely chopped carrot
   1 tablespoon finely chopped onion
   3 tablespoons mayonnaise or salad dressing
   2 teaspoons lemon juice
   2 teaspoons sugar
   ½ teaspoon salt
   ⅛ teaspoon pepper

4 to 6 servings

In medium bowl, combine cabbage, fish, carrot and onion. In small bowl or 1-cup measure, mix mayonnaise, lemon juice, sugar, salt and pepper. Pour dressing over salad, tossing gently to coat. Refrigerate at least 1 hour before serving.

Tossed Spinach Salad

½ pound walleye fillet, about ½-inch thick

MARINADE:
½ cup water
2 green onions, cut into 2-inch pieces
1 teaspoon soy sauce
½ teaspoon salt
¼ teaspoon sesame oil
⅛ teaspoon ground ginger
   Dash garlic powder

SALAD:
½ medium green pepper
2 cups torn fresh spinach
1 cup fresh bean sprouts
½ cup diagonally sliced celery
½ cup sliced fresh mushrooms
4 cherry tomatoes, cut in half

DRESSING:
⅓ cup vegetable oil
¼ cup white wine vinegar
½ teaspoon sugar
½ teaspoon soy sauce
¼ teaspoon salt
⅛ teaspoon sesame oil
   Dash ground ginger
   Dash pepper
1 tablespoon toasted sesame seed, optional

4 to 6 servings

Cut fillet into 1-inch chunks. Place in small bowl. In small saucepan, blend marinade ingredients. Heat to boiling. Pour over fish, stirring to coat. Cover by placing plastic wrap directly on surface of fish. Refrigerate at least 1 hour.

In small skillet, cook fish and marinade over medium heat, stirring gently, until fish flakes easily, 4 to 7 minutes. Remove fish with slotted spoon to paper towel-lined plate. Refrigerate about 30 minutes, until cool. Discard marinade and onions.

Cut green pepper into 2½ × ¼-inch strips. In medium bowl, combine green pepper strips, spinach, bean sprouts, celery, mushrooms and tomatoes. Add fish chunks. In small bowl, blend dressing ingredients. Pour dressing over salad, tossing gently to coat. Serve immediately.

NOTE: To toast sesame seed, cook in small skillet over medium-high heat, stirring constantly, until light brown, 2 to 3 minutes.

Fish Creole Salad ↑

½ cup thinly sliced celery
¼ cup chopped onion
¼ cup chopped green pepper
2 tablespoons margarine or butter
1 can (16 ounces) whole tomatoes
¼ cup white wine
1 teaspoon Worcestershire sauce
1 bay leaf
¼ teaspoon salt
⅛ teaspoon cayenne
   Dash garlic powder
½ pound walleye fillet, about ½-inch thick
5 to 6 cups torn iceberg lettuce

4 to 6 servings

In 10-inch skillet, cook and stir celery, onion and green pepper in margarine over medium heat until tender. Add tomatoes, wine, Worcestershire sauce, bay leaf, salt, cayenne and garlic powder. Heat to boiling. Reduce heat. Simmer, stirring occasionally and breaking up tomatoes, for 10 minutes.

Cut fillet into 1-inch pieces. Stir into tomato mixture. Cook over medium heat, stirring gently, until fish flakes easily, 5 to 7 minutes. Remove bay leaf. Serve over lettuce.

Salmon Louis ↑

DRESSING:
½ cup mayonnaise or salad dressing
3 tablespoons catsup
2 tablespoons dairy sour cream
2 tablespoons half-and-half
1 tablespoon chopped green onion
2 teaspoons chopped sweet pickle
1 teaspoon fresh lemon juice
½ teaspoon Worcestershire sauce

SALAD:
4 cups torn iceberg lettuce
2 cups flaked cooked salmon
1 tomato, cut into wedges
1 hard-cooked egg, sliced, optional
¼ cup sliced black olives, optional

4 to 6 servings

In small bowl, blend dressing ingredients. Refrigerate at least 30 minutes. Arrange lettuce in medium bowl or on serving plate. Mound fish in center. Arrange tomato wedges, egg slices and olives around fish. Pour half of dressing over salad. Reserve remaining dressing for serving.

Molded Waldorf Salad

1 to 1½ cups flaked cooked bass or other lean fish (page 34)
1 can (8 ounces) crushed pineapple, drained and ¼ cup juice reserved
⅔ cup chopped celery
1 medium red apple, cored and chopped
1 envelope unflavored gelatin
1 tablespoon cold water
¾ cup boiling water
1 tablespoon sugar
1 tablespoon lemon juice
1 cup mayonnaise or salad dressing

6 to 8 servings

Lightly oil 4- to 6-cup mold. In medium bowl, combine fish, crushed pineapple, celery and apple. In small bowl, mix gelatin with cold water. Stir in boiling water, mixing until gelatin dissolves. Stir in reserved pineapple juice, sugar and lemon juice, mixing until sugar dissolves. Blend in mayonnaise until smooth. Stir into fish, pineapple, celery and apple. Pour into prepared mold. Refrigerate about 4 hours, until firm.

Unmold onto serving plate lined with lettuce leaves. Garnish with apple slices, if desired.

Fish Soups & Chowders

Fish soups can be light and delicate, or rich and hearty. Serve them as a first course or as a complete one-dish meal.

Make soup from fresh or frozen fish, or from cooked leftovers. Watch the soup carefully after adding the fish, because it can easily overcook. Refrigerate leftover soup for use within 2 days, or freeze in plastic containers and use within a month.

← Hearty Vegetable and Panfish Soup

    4 slices bacon, cut up
    1 medium onion, chopped
    1 small green pepper, chopped
 ¼ cup chopped celery
    1 clove garlic, minced
    4 tomatoes, peeled and chopped
    2 cups sliced fresh mushrooms
    2 cups water
    1 can (6 ounces) tomato paste
 ½ cup white wine
    1 tablespoon plus 1 teaspoon instant chicken
       bouillon granules
    1 bay leaf
 ½ teaspoon dried oregano leaves
 ½ teaspoon sugar
 ¼ teaspoon ground sage
    1 pound panfish fillets

4 to 6 servings

In Dutch oven, cook bacon over medium-high heat, stirring occasionally, until crisp. Remove with slotted spoon; set aside. Add onion, green pepper, celery and garlic. Cook and stir over medium heat until vegetables are tender, 6 to 7 minutes. Add bacon and remaining ingredients except fish. Simmer, stirring occasionally, for 30 minutes. Cut fillets into 1-inch pieces. Add to soup. Simmer, stirring gently, until fish flakes easily, about 8 minutes.

Trout Gumbo

    3 slices bacon, cut up
    2 medium onions, chopped
 ½ cup chopped celery
    1 clove garlic, minced
    1 quart hot water
    1 can (28 ounces) whole tomatoes
    1 package (10 ounces) frozen whole okra
 ⅓ cup uncooked long-grain rice
    1 tablespoon fresh lemon juice
 1½ teaspoons instant chicken bouillon granules
    1 teaspoon salt
 ½ teaspoon dried basil leaves
 ⅛ to ¼ teaspoon cayenne
 ⅛ teaspoon pepper
    1 small bay leaf
    1 pound trout fillets

6 to 8 servings

In Dutch oven, cook bacon over medium-high heat, stirring occasionally, until crisp. Remove with slotted spoon; set aside. Add onion, celery and garlic. Cook and stir over medium heat until vegetables are tender-crisp, about 4 minutes.

Add bacon and remaining ingredients except fish. Heat to boiling. Reduce heat. Cover and simmer until rice is tender, 20 minutes. Cut fillets into 1-inch pieces. Add to soup. Cook over medium heat, stirring gently, until fish flakes easily, about 6 minutes.

Walleye Noodle Soup

    2 medium carrots
    1 stalk celery
    1 quart water
    1 small onion, cut into thin wedges
 ¼ cup snipped fresh parsley
    2 teaspoons instant chicken bouillon granules
 ½ teaspoon salt
 ¼ teaspoon dried thyme leaves
 ⅛ teaspoon pepper
 ½ cup uncooked narrow egg noodles
    1 cup flaked cooked walleye or other lean fish
       (page 34)

4 to 6 servings

Cut carrots into thin diagonal slices. Cut celery into thin slices. In 2-quart saucepan, combine water, carrots, celery, onion, parsley, bouillon granules, salt, thyme and pepper. Heat to boiling. Reduce heat. Cover and simmer 10 minutes. Add noodles; return to boiling. Cook until noodles are tender, 8 to 10 minutes. Stir in fish. Simmer for 1 minute.

Hot and Sour Bass Soup

← Hot and Sour Bass Soup

5 cups water
2 tablespoons instant chicken bouillon granules
¼ cup white vinegar
1 medium onion, cut into thin wedges
8 whole peppercorns
¾ pound bass fillets, about ½-inch thick
1 can (4 ounces) sliced mushrooms, drained
1 tablespoon soy sauce
1 clove garlic, minced
¼ to ½ teaspoon dried crushed red pepper
2 tablespoons cornstarch
2 tablespoons cold water
1 egg, beaten
1 green onion, chopped

4 to 6 servings

In Dutch oven, combine 5 cups water, the bouillon granules, vinegar, onion and peppercorns. Heat to boiling. Add fillets. Reduce heat. Cover and simmer until fish flakes easily, about 5 minutes. Remove fish. Cut into 1-inch pieces; set aside. Remove peppercorns. Stir mushrooms, soy sauce, garlic and red pepper into soup. Heat to boiling. Reduce heat. Cover and simmer for 15 minutes.

In small bowl, blend cornstarch into 2 tablespoons water. Stir into soup. Heat to boiling. Cook, stirring constantly, until soup is thickened, about 1 minute. Add fish. Reduce heat and simmer for 1 minute. Remove from heat. Pour beaten egg slowly in thin stream over soup; do not stir. Top with green onion.

Herbed Walleye Soup

1 medium onion, cut into thin wedges
1 clove garlic, minced
2 tablespoons margarine or butter
2 cups hot water
1 tablespoon instant chicken bouillon granules
1 cup white wine
¼ teaspoon dried thyme leaves
¼ teaspoon dried basil leaves
¼ teaspoon pepper
⅛ teaspoon dried rosemary leaves
¾ pound walleye fillets, skin on

6 to 8 servings

In 3-quart saucepan, cook and stir onion and garlic in margarine over medium heat until onion is tender, about 7 minutes.

Blend the hot water and bouillon granules into onions. Add remaining ingredients except fish. Heat to boiling. Reduce heat. Cover and simmer, stirring occasionally, for 30 minutes.

Cut fillets into 1-inch pieces; add to soup. Simmer, stirring occasionally, until fish flakes easily, about 10 minutes. Skim fat, if desired.

Fish and Citrus Soup

¾ pound panfish fillets
2 tablespoons soy sauce
1 medium onion, chopped
2 cloves garlic, minced
2 tablespoons olive or vegetable oil
2¼ cups water
¼ cup fresh orange juice
¼ cup fresh lemon juice
1½ teaspoons instant chicken bouillon granules
1 teaspoon grated orange rind
1 teaspoon grated lemon rind
1 teaspoon sugar
⅛ teaspoon pepper

4 to 6 servings

Cut fillets into 1-inch pieces. In small bowl, mix fish and soy sauce. Cover and refrigerate at least 1 hour, stirring once to keep fish pieces coated.

In 2-quart saucepan, cook and stir onion and garlic in olive oil over medium heat until tender, about 3 minutes. Add remaining ingredients except fish. Heat to boiling. Reduce heat and simmer for 5 minutes. Add fish and soy sauce. Simmer, stirring gently, until fish flakes easily, about 8 minutes.

Bouillabaisse →

1 medium green pepper, chopped
1 medium onion, chopped
2 cloves garlic, minced
2 tablespoons olive or vegetable oil
3 cups fish stock (page 26)*
1 cup clam-tomato juice cocktail
1 can (16 ounces) whole tomatoes
½ teaspoon sugar
½ teaspoon salt
¼ teaspoon dried thyme leaves
¼ teaspoon ground turmeric
⅛ teaspoon pepper
1 bay leaf
½ pound trout fillets, skin on
½ pound walleye or other lean fish fillets
   (page 34), skin on
½ pound raw shrimp, peeled and deveined
1 can (6½ ounces) minced clams, drained

6 to 8 servings

In Dutch oven, cook and stir green pepper, onion and garlic in olive oil over medium heat until onion is tender, about 4 minutes. Add fish stock, clam-tomato juice, tomatoes, sugar, salt, thyme, turmeric, pepper and bay leaf. Heat to boiling. Reduce heat. Cover and simmer, stirring occasionally to break up tomatoes, for 15 minutes.

Cut trout and walleye fillets into 1-inch pieces. Add fish, shrimp and clams to stew. Cook over medium heat, stirring gently, until fish flakes easily and shrimp turns opaque, about 5 minutes.

*Or, substitute 1 can (14½ ounces) ready-to-serve chicken broth and 1¼ cups water; omit the salt.

Cream of Salmon Soup

1 cup sliced fresh mushrooms
¼ cup finely chopped onion
¼ cup margarine or butter
3 tablespoons all-purpose flour
2 tablespoons snipped fresh parsley
½ teaspoon salt
⅛ teaspoon white pepper
⅛ teaspoon dried rosemary leaves
1½ cups milk
1½ cups half-and-half
1½ to 2 cups flaked cooked salmon

4 to 6 servings

In 2-quart saucepan, cook and stir mushrooms and onion in margarine over medium heat until just tender, about 5 minutes. Stir in flour, parsley, salt, pepper and rosemary. Remove from heat. Blend in milk and half-and-half. Cook over medium heat, stirring constantly, until thickened and bubbly, 7 to 10 minutes. Add fish. Cook and stir 1 minute.

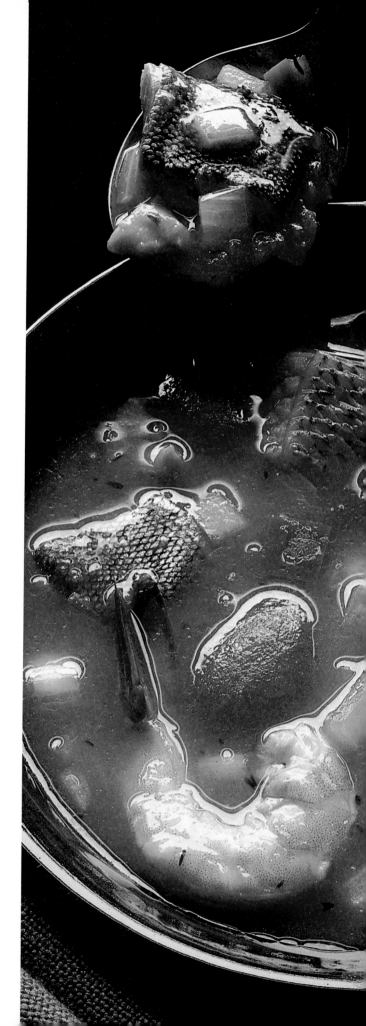

Creamy Tomato and Panfish Soup ↑

2 large red potatoes (about 1 pound)
1 medium onion, chopped
¼ cup chopped celery
3 tablespoons margarine or butter
2 cups water
1 can (16 ounces) whole tomatoes, drained
½ cup white wine
1 teaspoon salt
  Dash pepper
3 tablespoons all-purpose flour
¼ cup cold water
½ cup half-and-half
1 pound panfish fillets

4 to 6 servings

Peel potatoes; cut into ¼-inch cubes. Set aside. In 3-quart saucepan, cook and stir onion and celery in margarine over medium heat until tender-crisp, about 5 minutes. Add potato cubes, 2 cups water, the tomatoes, wine, salt and pepper. Blend flour into ¼ cup cold water; stir into vegetable mixture. Heat to boiling. Reduce heat. Cover and simmer, stirring occasionally, until potatoes are tender, 20 minutes. Stir in half-and-half. Cut fillets into 1-inch pieces. Add to soup. Cover and simmer, stirring gently one or two times, until fish flakes easily, about 8 minutes.

Panfish Chowder

6 slices bacon, cut up
3 medium red potatoes (about 1 pound)
⅔ cup chopped onion
½ cup chopped celery
2 cups fish stock (page 26)*
1 cup sliced fresh mushrooms
½ cup chopped carrot
¼ cup snipped fresh parsley
1 tablespoon fresh lemon or lime juice
1 teaspoon salt
½ teaspoon dried dillweed
⅛ teaspoon dried fennel seed
⅛ teaspoon garlic salt
⅛ teaspoon pepper
1 cup half-and-half
1½ cups cut-up cooked panfish
    (about 1½-inch pieces)

4 to 6 servings

In 3-quart saucepan, cook bacon over medium-high heat, stirring occasionally, until crisp. Remove with slotted spoon; set aside. Peel potatoes and cut into ¾-inch cubes; set aside.

Cook and stir onion and celery in bacon fat over medium-high heat until tender, about 5 minutes. Add bacon, potato cubes, fish stock, mushrooms, carrot, parsley, lemon juice, salt, dillweed, fennel seed, garlic salt and pepper. Heat to boiling. Reduce heat. Cover and simmer until vegetables are tender, 15 to 20 minutes. Blend in half-and-half. Gently stir in fish pieces. Skim fat, if desired.

*Or, substitute 2 cups water and 2 teaspoons instant chicken bouillon granules; omit the 1 teaspoon salt.

Tomato-Dill Fish Soup

3 cups water
1 teaspoon dried dillweed
½ teaspoon salt
  Dash pepper
1 pound muskie or other lean fish fillets
    (page 34), about ½-inch thick
1 can (10¾ ounces) condensed tomato soup
2 tablespoons margarine or butter

4 to 6 servings

In Dutch oven, combine water, dillweed, salt and pepper. Heat to boiling. Add fillets. Reduce heat. Cover and simmer until fish flakes easily, about 5 minutes. Remove fish with slotted spatula.

Add tomato soup and margarine to cooking liquid. Cook over medium heat until bubbly, about 4 minutes. Cut fish into bite-size pieces. Reduce heat. Gently stir fish into soup. Simmer for 2 minutes.

Country Trout Chowder ↑

1 small onion
½ cup chopped celery
2 tablespoons margarine or butter
2 small zucchini (about ½ pound)
3 cups fish stock (page 26)*
2 cups coarsely chopped cabbage
1 can (15 ounces) Northern beans, drained
2 tablespoons snipped fresh parsley
1 tablespoon fresh lemon juice
½ teaspoon salt
4 whole peppercorns
1¼ pounds trout steaks, about 1-inch thick
   Thin lemon wedges

4 to 6 servings

Cut onion into thin slices and separate into rings. In Dutch oven, cook and stir onion and celery in margarine over medium heat until onion is tender, about 5 minutes.

Cut zucchini into ½-inch slices. Add zucchini, fish stock and remaining ingredients except fish and lemon wedges to onion and celery. Heat to boiling. Reduce heat. Cover and simmer, stirring occasionally, until zucchini is tender, 6 to 8 minutes.

Add fish to soup. Simmer, stirring gently one or two times, until fish flakes easily, about 10 minutes. Garnish with lemon wedges; squeeze juice over chowder before eating.

*Or, substitute 1 can (14½ ounces) ready-to-serve chicken broth and 1¼ cups water; omit the ½ teaspoon salt.

New England Chowder

1 quart water
1 teaspoon salt
4 large red potatoes (about 2 pounds)
1 pound bass or other lean fish fillets (page 34)
6 slices bacon, cut up
1 small onion, chopped
¼ cup all-purpose flour
½ teaspoon salt
⅛ teaspoon pepper
⅛ teaspoon dried thyme leaves
3 cups milk
1 small bay leaf
2 cups half-and-half

6 to 8 servings

In 2-quart saucepan, heat water and 1 teaspoon salt to boiling. Add potatoes. Return to boiling. Reduce heat. Cover and simmer until tender, 25 to 35 minutes. Drain; cool. Peel and cut into ½-inch cubes. Set aside. Cut fillets into 1-inch pieces; set aside.

In Dutch oven, cook bacon over medium-high heat, stirring occasionally, until crisp. Remove with slotted spoon; set aside. Add onion. Cook and stir until tender, about 2 minutes. Reduce to medium heat. Stir in flour, ½ teaspoon salt, the pepper and thyme. Add bacon. Blend in milk. Add bay leaf. Cook over medium heat, stirring constantly, until thickened and bubbly. Reduce heat to low. Blend in half-and-half. Stir in potato cubes and fish. Cook over low heat, stirring gently, until fish flakes easily, about 12 minutes. Garnish each serving with chopped chives, if desired.

Main Dishes

Fish is easy to prepare but the cooking time should be carefully watched. Test for doneness before the time given in the recipe. A perfectly cooked fish is moist and flaky.

The whole fish used in these recipes are drawn (see Field Dressing, page 8). This means they are gutted and gilled, but the head, fins and tail are retained.

← Rye-Stuffed Trout

  4 slices rye bread
⅓ cup chopped celery
  2 tablespoons chopped onion
  1 teaspoon grated orange peel
¼ cup margarine or butter
  2 tablespoons fresh orange juice
¼ cup snipped fresh parsley
¼ cup coarsely chopped cashews or peanuts
  4 small drawn trout, about ½ pound each

4 servings

Set oven to broil and/or 550°. Cut bread into ½-inch cubes. Spread bread cubes on baking sheet. Broil 5 to 6 inches from heat, stirring one or two times, until toasted, about 4 minutes. Set aside. Set oven to bake and/or 375°. Grease 13×9-inch baking pan.

In 1½-quart saucepan, cook and stir celery, onion and orange peel in margarine over medium heat until tender, about 5 minutes. Stir in orange juice. Heat until bubbly. Stir in parsley and nuts. Add bread cubes; toss to coat. Remove from heat.

Place fish in prepared pan. Stuff with bread mixture. If desired, brush fish with 2 tablespoons melted margarine or butter before baking. Bake until fish flakes easily at backbone, about 20 minutes.

Deep-Fried Catfish

     Vegetable oil
½ cup buttermilk
¾ cup yellow cornmeal
1½ to 2 pounds small whole catfish or bullhead,
     head and skin removed

4 servings

In deep-fat fryer or saucepan, heat oil (2 to 3 inches) to 375°. Pour buttermilk into shallow dish or pie plate. Sprinkle cornmeal on plate or waxed paper. Dip fish into buttermilk. Coat with cornmeal. Fry a few pieces at a time, turning over one or two times, until deep golden brown, about 4 minutes. Drain on paper towels. Keep warm in 175° oven. Repeat with remaining fish.

← Vegetable Stuffed Walleye

1 medium zucchini
1 small onion, thinly sliced
1 cup sliced fresh mushrooms
3 thin lemon slices
2 tablespoons olive or vegetable oil
2 tablespoons margarine or butter
2 tablespoons grated Parmesan cheese
¼ teaspoon pepper
⅛ teaspoon garlic powder
2 to 3-pound drawn walleye
2 tablespoons margarine or butter, melted

4 to 6 servings

Heat oven to 375°. Grease 13 × 9-inch baking pan. Cut zucchini in half lengthwise, then into thin slices. In 9-inch skillet, cook and stir zucchini, onion, mushrooms and lemon slices in olive oil and 2 tablespoons margarine over medium heat until tender, about 3 minutes. Remove lemon slices; set aside. Stir Parmesan cheese, pepper and garlic powder into vegetables.

Place fish in prepared pan. Stuff with vegetable mixture, placing any extra stuffing around fish. Brush fish with melted margarine. Place lemon slices on top of fish. Bake until fish flakes easily at backbone, 30 to 35 minutes.

Walleye With Rice Stuffing

1 package (6 ounces) wild and long grain rice mix
1 teaspoon instant chicken bouillon granules
1½ cups sliced fresh mushrooms
½ cup chopped celery
2 tablespoons margarine or butter
1 jar (2 ounces) sliced pimiento, drained
⅛ teaspoon ground sage
2 to 2½-pound drawn walleye

4 to 6 servings

Prepare rice as directed on package, adding bouillon granules to water. Set aside. Heat oven to 375°. Grease broiler pan or 13 × 9-inch baking pan.

In small skillet, cook and stir mushrooms and celery in margarine over medium heat until mushrooms are tender, about 5 minutes. Stir in pimiento and sage. Stir vegetables into rice.

Place walleye on broiler pan. Stuff with rice mixture, placing any extra stuffing around fish. Cover rice only with foil. Bake until fish flakes easily at backbone, 20 to 25 minutes. If desired, serve with Citrus Butter, page 140.

Lemon-Cucumber Stuffed Trout →

½ cup chopped, seeded, peeled cucumber
½ cup shredded carrot
2 tablespoons chopped onion
½ teaspoon lemon pepper
¼ cup margarine or butter
½ cup hot water
1 teaspoon instant chicken bouillon granules
2 tablespoons snipped fresh parsley
3 cups dry bread cubes
4 small drawn trout, about ½ pound each

4 servings

Heat oven to 375°. Grease 13 × 9-inch baking pan. In small skillet, cook and stir cucumber, carrot, onion and lemon pepper in margarine over medium heat until tender, about 6 minutes. Blend in water and bouillon granules. Heat to boiling. Add parsley. Remove from heat.

In medium bowl, stir bread cubes into vegetables until coated. Place fish in prepared pan. Stuff each trout with one-fourth of bread mixture. If desired, brush fish with 2 tablespoons melted margarine or butter before baking. Bake until fish flakes easily at backbone, about 20 minutes.

Wild Rice Stuffed Trout

1 cup uncooked wild rice
2½ cups hot water
1 teaspoon salt
⅓ cup chopped water chestnuts
¼ cup chopped green onions
1 tablespoon chopped stuffed green olives
3 tablespoons margarine or butter
4 small drawn trout, about ½ pound each

4 servings

Rinse and drain rice. In 3-quart saucepan, combine rice, water and salt. Heat to boiling, stirring one or two times. Reduce heat. Cover and simmer until rice is tender, 40 to 50 minutes, checking one or two times to be sure rice is not sticking. Add a few tablespoons water, if necessary. Set aside.

Heat oven to 375°. Grease 13 × 9-inch baking pan. In small skillet, cook and stir water chestnuts, green onions and olives in margarine over medium heat for 2 minutes. Stir into rice.

Place trout in prepared pan. Stuff with wild rice. If desired, brush fish with 2 tablespoons melted margarine or butter before baking. Bake until fish flakes easily at backbone, about 20 minutes.

Baked Walleye and Ratatouille ↑

1 medium onion
2 cloves garlic, minced
¼ cup olive or vegetable oil
1 eggplant (about 1 pound)
3 medium zucchini (about 1 pound)
1 medium green pepper
2 cups sliced fresh mushrooms
1 can (16 ounces) whole tomatoes, drained, cut up
1 teaspoon salt
¾ teaspoon dried basil leaves
½ teaspoon dried oregano leaves
¼ teaspoon pepper
2 to 3-pound drawn walleye

2 to 4 servings

Heat oven to 350°. Cut onion into thin slices and separate into rings. In Dutch oven, cook and stir onion and garlic in olive oil over medium heat until onion is tender, about 5 minutes. Peel eggplant and cut into ¾-inch cubes. Cut zucchini into ¼-inch slices. Core and seed green pepper; cut into ½-inch strips. Stir eggplant, zucchini, green pepper, mushrooms, tomatoes, salt, basil, oregano and pepper into onions. Cook over medium heat, stirring occasionally, for 10 minutes. Set aside.

Place fish on large sheet of heavy-duty aluminum foil. Spoon vegetables over and around fish. Wrap tightly. Place on baking sheet. Bake until fish flakes easily at backbone, about 35 minutes.

Bullheads Marinated in Barbecue Sauce

3 tablespoons chopped onion
1 tablespoon olive or vegetable oil
¼ cup packed dark brown sugar
¼ cup catsup
¼ cup cider vinegar
2 tablespoons Worcestershire sauce
½ teaspoon dry mustard
¼ teaspoon salt
¼ teaspoon pepper
⅛ teaspoon dried oregano leaves
1½ to 2 pounds small whole bullheads, heads and skin removed

4 to 6 servings

In small skillet, cook and stir onion in olive oil over medium heat until tender, about 3 minutes. Stir in brown sugar, catsup, vinegar, Worcestershire sauce, dry mustard, salt, pepper and oregano. Cook, stirring occasionally, until bubbly. Reduce heat. Simmer, stirring occasionally, for 10 minutes.

Place fish in medium bowl. Pour marinade over fish; cover. Refrigerate at least 30 minutes, turning fish over once. Set oven to broil and/or 550°. Grease broiler pan. With slotted spoon, remove fish from bowl and place on pan. Baste with marinade. Broil 4 to 5 inches from heat for 8 minutes; turn. Baste with marinade. Broil until fish flakes easily at backbone, about 7 minutes.

Sesame-Dill Broiled Salmon ↑

1 tablespoon sesame seed
1 teaspoon dried dillweed
3 tablespoons margarine or butter
¼ teaspoon salt
⅛ teaspoon pepper
4 salmon steaks, about 1-inch thick

4 servings

Set oven to broil and/or 550°. Grease broiler pan. In small skillet, cook and stir sesame seed and dillweed in margarine over medium heat until sesame seed is light brown, about 4 minutes. Stir in salt and pepper. Remove from heat.

Place fish on broiler pan. Brush with half of sesame seed mixture. Broil 5 to 6 inches from heat for 5 minutes; turn. Brush with remaining sesame seed mixture. Broil until fish flakes easily in center, about 5 minutes.

Sherry Poached Salmon

2½ quarts hot water
1 cup sherry
1 stalk celery, cut into 1-inch pieces
½ teaspoon dried bouquet garni seasoning
½ teaspoon garlic salt
⅛ teaspoon whole peppercorns
4 salmon steaks, about 1-inch thick
Sherried White Sauce Variation (page 141)

4 servings

In fish poacher or Dutch oven, combine water, sherry, celery, bouquet garni, garlic salt and peppercorns. Heat to boiling. Reduce heat. Cover and simmer for 15 minutes.

Lower fish into simmering liquid. Fish should be covered; add boiling water as needed. Cover poacher. Simmer until fish flakes easily in center, about 10 minutes. Remove from liquid. Prepare Sherried White Sauce as directed. Spoon over fish.

← Marinated Salmon Steaks

½ cup vegetable oil
½ cup white wine vinegar
1 teaspoon sugar
1 teaspoon dried parsley flakes
½ teaspoon dried Italian seasoning
¼ teaspoon garlic salt
¼ teaspoon onion powder
⅛ teaspoon paprika
⅛ teaspoon pepper
4 salmon steaks, about 1-inch thick

4 servings

In shallow bowl, blend oil, vinegar, sugar, parsley flakes, Italian seasoning, garlic salt, onion powder, paprika and pepper. Place fish in plastic bag. Pour marinade over fish. Seal bag. Refrigerate 1½ hours, turning bag over two or three times.

Set oven to broil and/or 550°. Grease broiler pan. Remove fish from marinade. Reserve marinade. Arrange fish on broiler pan; baste with marinade. Broil 4 to 5 inches from heat for 5 minutes; turn. Baste with remaining marinade. Broil until fish flakes easily in center, about 5 minutes.

Crunchy Oriental Fillets

½ cup water
⅓ cup teriyaki sauce
½ teaspoon ground ginger
  Dash dry mustard
1 pound panfish or other lean fish fillets
  (page 34), ¼- to ½-inch thick
3 cups chow mein noodles, crushed
¼ cup margarine or butter, melted
½ cup dairy sour cream
2½ teaspoons soy sauce
⅛ teaspoon ground ginger
1 tablespoon finely chopped green onion

2 to 4 servings

In small dish, combine water, teriyaki sauce, ½ teaspoon ginger and the dry mustard. Cut fish into serving-size pieces. Place in plastic bag. Pour marinade over fish. Seal bag. Refrigerate at least 30 minutes, turning bag over one or two times. Drain and discard marinade.

Heat oven to 375°. Grease 13 × 9-inch baking pan. Sprinkle chow mein noodles on plate or waxed paper. Dip fillets in melted margarine. Coat with crushed chow mein noodles, pressing lightly. Place in prepared pan. Bake until fish flakes easily at thickest part, 15 to 20 minutes.

In small dish, blend sour cream, soy sauce and ⅛ teaspoon ginger. Spoon over baked fish. Top with green onion.

Almond Fried Trout ↑

¼ cup all-purpose flour
⅛ teaspoon pepper
1 egg
3 tablespoons milk
1 cup cracker crumbs
½ cup sliced almonds, coarsely chopped
1½ pounds trout fillets, about ½-inch thick
2 tablespoons margarine or butter
¼ cup plus 1 tablespoon vegetable oil

4 servings

Heat oven to 450°. On plate or waxed paper, mix flour and pepper. In shallow dish or pie plate, blend egg and milk. On another plate or waxed paper, mix cracker crumbs and almonds. Cut fish into serving-size pieces. Coat fish with flour, dip in egg, then coat with almond mixture, pressing lightly.

In 13 × 9-inch baking pan, combine margarine and oil. Place pan in oven for 5 minutes to heat oil. Add fish, turning to coat with oil. Bake 5 minutes. Turn fish. Bake until fish is golden brown and flakes easily at thickest part, about 5 minutes. Drain on paper towels. Serve with lemon wedges, if desired.

Tempura Fried Walleye

1 egg, separated
1 cup very cold water
1 cup all-purpose flour
¼ teaspoon salt
¾ teaspoon sesame oil, optional
  Vegetable oil
1½ pounds walleye or other lean fish fillets
  (page 34), about ½-inch thick
1 cup fresh parsley sprigs, optional

4 to 6 servings

In medium bowl, blend egg yolk and water. Blend in flour, salt and sesame oil until smooth; cover. Refrigerate at least 30 minutes. (Do not refrigerate egg white.) In small bowl, beat egg white until stiff peaks form. Gently fold into chilled batter.

In deep-fat fryer or deep skillet, heat oil (1½ to 3 inches) to 375°. Cut fish into serving-size pieces. Dip fish into chilled batter. Fry a few pieces at a time, turning over one or two times, until light golden brown, about 3 minutes. Drain on paper towels. Keep warm in 175° oven.

With slotted spoon, dip one-fourth of the parsley in the remaining batter. Fry, turning over once, until light golden brown, about 45 seconds. Repeat with remaining parsley. Serve with fish.

Potato Chip Coated Fillets

⅓ cup buttermilk
⅛ teaspoon pepper
1 bag (4 ounces) potato chips, crushed
¾ cup cornflake crumbs
¼ teaspoon paprika
1½ pounds northern pike or other lean fish
    fillets (page 34), about ½-inch thick

4 to 6 servings

In shallow dish or pie plate, mix buttermilk and pepper. On plate or waxed paper, mix crushed potato chips, cornflake crumbs and paprika. Set oven to broil and/or 550°. Grease broiler pan.

Cut fish into serving-size pieces. Dip in buttermilk. Coat with potato chip mixture, pressing lightly. Place on broiler pan. Broil 6 inches from heat for 3 minutes; turn. Broil until fish flakes easily at thickest part, 2 to 3 minutes.

Crunchy Fried Walleye

1 egg
1 cup evaporated milk
2 cups cracker crumbs
⅛ teaspoon salt
⅛ teaspoon pepper
1½ pounds walleye or other lean fish fillets
    (page 34), about ½-inch thick
2 to 4 tablespoons vegetable oil

4 to 6 servings

In shallow dish or pie plate, blend egg and milk. On plate or waxed paper, combine cracker crumbs, salt and pepper. Cut fish into serving-size pieces. Dip in milk. Coat with cracker crumbs.

In 9-inch skillet, heat oil. Fry a few pieces at a time until golden brown, about 3 minutes; turn. Fry until golden brown, 1½ to 3 minutes. Drain on paper towels. Keep warm in 175° oven. Repeat with remaining fish.

Parmesan Bass Fillets

1½ pounds bass or other lean fish fillets
    (page 34), about ¾-inch thick
¼ cup margarine or butter
½ teaspoon salt
⅛ teaspoon pepper
1 tablespoon fresh lemon juice
1 tablespoon white wine
3 tablespoons grated Parmesan cheese
    Paprika

4 to 6 servings

Heat oven to 450°. Cut fish into serving-size pieces. Place margarine in 13×9-inch baking pan. Place pan in oven for 5 minutes to melt margarine. Place fish in pan, skin side up. Sprinkle with salt and pepper. Bake for 5 minutes; turn. Sprinkle with lemon juice and white wine. Top with Parmesan cheese. Sprinkle with paprika. Bake until fish flakes easily at thickest part, about 5 minutes.

Lemon Fried Panfish

1 cup all-purpose flour
2 teaspoons grated lemon peel
½ teaspoon salt
¼ teaspoon pepper
1 cup water
    Vegetable oil
1½ pounds panfish or other lean fish fillets
    (page 34)
    All-purpose flour

4 to 6 servings

In medium bowl, combine 1 cup flour, the lemon peel, salt and pepper. Blend in water; cover. Refrigerate at least 30 minutes.

In deep-fat fryer or deep skillet, heat oil (1½ to 3 inches) to 375°. Coat fish with flour, then dip in chilled batter. Fry a few pieces at a time, turning occasionally, until light golden brown, about 3 minutes. Drain on paper towels. Keep warm in 175° oven. Repeat with remaining fish.

Tomato Baked Walleye Fillets ↑

1 medium onion
2 tablespoons olive or vegetable oil
1½ pounds walleye or other lean fish fillets
    (page 34), about ½-inch thick
1½ cups sliced fresh mushrooms
1 can (7½ ounces) whole tomatoes,
    drained, cut up
⅓ cup white wine
½ teaspoon salt
⅛ teaspoon pepper
⅛ teaspoon garlic powder
1 medium tomato, thinly sliced
½ teaspoon dried oregano leaves
2 tablespoons snipped fresh parsley

4 to 6 servings

Cut onion into thin slices and separate into rings. In 9-inch skillet, cook and stir onion in olive oil over medium heat until tender-crisp, about 5 minutes. Set aside.

Heat oven to 350°. Place fish in 13 × 9-inch baking pan. Top with onion rings. Sprinkle mushrooms over onions. Set aside.

In small bowl, combine canned tomatoes, wine, salt, pepper and garlic powder. Spoon evenly over fish and vegetables. Top with tomato slices. Sprinkle oregano and parsley over tomato. Bake until fish flakes easily at thickest part, 25 to 30 minutes.

Herbed Northern Pike and Vegetables

2 medium zucchini (about ½ pound)
¼ pound fresh broccoli
1 small onion, cut into thin wedges
½ cup thinly sliced celery
¼ cup thinly sliced carrot
2 tablespoons olive or vegetable oil
1½ pounds northern pike or other lean
    fish fillets (page 34), about ½-inch thick
2 tablespoons margarine or butter
¼ teaspoon dried basil leaves
¼ teaspoon salt
⅛ teaspoon dried rosemary leaves
⅛ teaspoon garlic salt
⅛ teaspoon pepper
    Paprika

4 to 6 servings

Cut zucchini into 2 × ½-inch strips. Chop broccoli. In 9-inch skillet, cook and stir zucchini, broccoli, onion, celery and carrot in olive oil over medium heat until tender-crisp, about 10 minutes. Spread evenly on broiler pan. Cut fish into serving-size pieces. Arrange on top of vegetables.

Set oven to broil and/or 550°. In ½-quart saucepan, melt margarine. Stir in basil, salt, rosemary, garlic salt and pepper. Brush on fish.

Broil 5 to 6 inches from heat until fish flakes easily at thickest part, 5 to 8 minutes. Sprinkle with paprika before serving.

Cheesy Northern Pike Bake

1 pound fresh broccoli
1 pound fresh cauliflower
   (about ½ medium head)
1 quart water
½ teaspoon salt
½ cup thinly sliced carrot
2 tablespoons margarine or butter
2 tablespoons all-purpose flour
½ teaspoon salt
⅛ teaspoon dry mustard
⅛ teaspoon white pepper
   Dash cayenne
1 cup milk
¾ cup shredded Cheddar cheese
1½ pounds northern pike or other lean fish fillets
   (page 34), about ½-inch thick, skin removed
2 tablespoons margarine or butter, melted
½ cup fine dry bread crumbs
⅛ teaspoon paprika

4 to 6 servings

Cut broccoli stems into ¾-inch thick slices; separate tops into flowerets. Separate cauliflower into flowerets. In 3-quart saucepan, heat water and ½ teaspoon salt to boiling. Add broccoli, cauliflower and carrot; cover. Cook over high heat for 5 minutes. Drain. Rinse under cold running water; drain well. Set aside.

In 1-quart saucepan, melt 2 tablespoons margarine over medium heat. Stir in flour, ½ teaspoon salt, the dry mustard, white pepper and cayenne. Blend in milk. Cook over medium heat, stirring constantly, until thickened and bubbly, about 4 minutes. Stir in cheese until melted. Remove from heat. Set aside.

Heat oven to 325°. Grease 13×9-inch baking pan. Place vegetables in pan. Evenly spread half of the cheese sauce over the vegetables. Cut fish into serving-size pieces. Place on vegetables. Evenly spread remaining cheese sauce over fish. Set aside.

In small dish, mix 2 tablespoons melted margarine, the bread crumbs and paprika. Sprinkle over cheese sauce. Bake until fish flakes easily at thickest part, 25 to 30 minutes.

← Sour Cream Fish Bake

    1 quart water
    1 teaspoon salt
    4 large red potatoes (about 2 pounds)
    6 slices bacon, cut up
1½ pounds northern pike or other lean fish fillets
       (page 34), about ½-inch thick
    1 medium onion
    1 medium green pepper
1½ cups dairy sour cream
   ½ cup half-and-half
   2 teaspoons dried chopped chives
   ½ teaspoon salt
   ⅛ teaspoon pepper
   ¼ cup snipped fresh parsley

6 to 8 servings

In 2-quart saucepan, heat water and 1 teaspoon salt to boiling. Add potatoes. Return to boiling. Reduce heat. Cover and simmer until potatoes are fork tender, about 30 minutes. Drain. Cool and slice.

In small skillet, cook and stir bacon over medium-high heat until brown, but not crisp, about 7 minutes. Drain, reserving 2 tablespoons fat. Set bacon aside. Cut fish into serving-size pieces. Slice onion and separate into rings. Core and seed green pepper; cut into rings. Set aside.

Heat oven to 325°. Grease 13 × 9-inch baking pan. Layer potato slices in pan. Pour reserved bacon fat over potatoes.

In small bowl, blend sour cream, half-and-half, chives, ½ teaspoon salt and the pepper. Spoon one-third of mixture over potatoes. Layer fish and onion rings over sour cream and potatoes. Spoon on remaining sour cream. Top with green pepper rings, parsley and bacon. Bake until fish in center of pan flakes easily, about 1 hour.

Bass With Blue Cheese Sauce

    1 tablespoon all-purpose flour
    1 cup dairy sour cream
   ¾ cup white wine
    2 ounces blue cheese, crumbled
    1 tablespoon dried chopped chives
     Dash white pepper
1½ pounds bass or other lean fish fillets (page 34),
     ¼- to ½-inch thick

4 to 6 servings

Heat oven to 300°. Grease 13 × 9-inch baking pan. In small bowl, mix flour and sour cream. Blend in wine, cheese, chives and white pepper. Cut fish into serving-size pieces. Place in prepared pan. Spread with sauce. Bake until fish flakes easily at thickest part, 30 to 40 minutes. Place fish on warm serving plate. Stir sauce before serving.

Walleye in Creamy Orange Sauce ↑

2 tablespoons margarine or butter
2 tablespoons finely chopped onion
1 tablespoon all-purpose flour
1 teaspoon grated orange peel
¼ teaspoon salt
⅛ teaspoon pepper
1 cup half-and-half or milk
1½ pounds walleye or other lean fish fillets
    (page 34), about ½-inch thick

4 to 6 servings

Heat oven to 300°. Grease 13 × 9-inch baking pan. In small saucepan, melt margarine over medium heat. Stir in onion, flour, orange peel, salt and pepper. Blend in half-and-half. Cook over medium heat, stirring constantly, until thickened and bubbly, about 4 minutes. Set aside.

Cut fish into serving-size pieces. Place in prepared pan. Pour sauce over fish. Cover with foil. Bake until fish flakes easily at thickest part, about 25 minutes. Garnish with orange slices, if desired.

Marinated Bass Fillets

½ cup bottled creamy French dressing
2 tablespoons fresh lime juice
¼ teaspoon salt
⅛ teaspoon pepper
1½ pounds bass or other lean fish fillets
    (page 34), about ½-inch thick
1 can (3½ ounces) French-fried onion rings,
    coarsely crushed
⅓ cup grated Parmesan cheese
½ teaspoon dried parsley flakes

4 to 6 servings

In small bowl, blend French dressing, lime juice, salt and pepper. Cut fish into serving-size pieces. Place in a plastic bag. Add dressing mixture; seal. Refrigerate at least 30 minutes, turning over once.

Heat oven to 375°. Grease 13 × 9-inch baking pan. With slotted spoon, remove fish from marinade; place in pan. Mix onion rings, cheese and parsley. Sprinkle over fish. Bake until fish flakes easily at thickest part, about 20 minutes.

Florentine-Stuffed Northern Pike →

2 packages (10 ounces each) frozen chopped
    spinach, thawed
2 cups sliced fresh mushrooms
3 tablespoons olive or vegetable oil
1 cup ricotta cheese
1 egg, slightly beaten
⅓ cup herb-seasoned stuffing mix
¼ cup grated Parmesan cheese
1 jar (2 ounces) sliced pimiento, drained
½ teaspoon salt
¼ teaspoon pepper
¼ teaspoon dried basil leaves
⅛ teaspoon onion powder
2 northern pike or other lean fish fillets (page 34),
    1 pound each, about ¾-inch thick,
    skin removed
    Almondine Butter (page 140)
    Paprika

6 to 8 servings

How to Prepare Florentine-Stuffed Northern Pike

DRAIN thawed spinach in colander, pressing out excess moisture. Set aside. In 9-inch skillet, cook and stir mushrooms in olive oil over medium heat until tender, about 4 minutes.

COMBINE mushrooms, spinach, ricotta cheese, beaten egg, stuffing mix, Parmesan cheese, pimiento, salt, pepper, basil and onion powder in medium bowl. Mix well. Set aside.

HEAT oven to 325°. Grease broiler pan. Place one fillet on pan. Spread about half of the spinach stuffing on the fillet.

CUT a slit lengthwise through middle of other fillet, leaving 3 inches uncut on each end. Place on top of spinach and other fillet. Spoon remaining spinach stuffing in center of split fillet.

PREPARE Almondine Butter. Spoon half of butter over fish. Sprinkle with paprika. Bake until both fillets flake easily at thickest part, 35 to 40 minutes. Serve with remaining butter.

Vegetable-Dressed Fillets

½ cup chopped celery
⅓ cup chopped green pepper
¼ cup chopped onion
¼ cup thinly sliced carrot
¼ cup margarine or butter
1 medium tomato
1 cup dry bread cubes
1 tablespoon snipped fresh parsley
¼ teaspoon dried dillweed
¼ teaspoon salt
   Dash pepper
1½ pounds bass or other lean fish fillets (page 34),
   about ½-inch thick
2 tablespoons white wine

4 to 6 servings

Heat oven to 350°. Grease 13 × 9-inch baking pan. In small skillet, cook and stir celery, green pepper, onion and carrot in margarine over medium heat until tender, about 5 minutes. Set aside.

Peel and seed tomato; chop. In small bowl, combine tomato, bread cubes, parsley, dillweed, salt and pepper. Add vegetables. Set aside.

Cut fish into serving-size pieces. Arrange in prepared pan. Cover fillets evenly with vegetable mixture. Sprinkle with wine. Bake until fish flakes easily at thickest part, about 25 minutes.

Spicy Poached Fish

1½ quarts hot water
1 medium onion, chopped
2 lemon slices
1 clove garlic, minced
2 teaspoons salt
½ teaspoon whole allspice
½ teaspoon whole cloves
¼ teaspoon dried crushed red pepper
1 bay leaf
1½ pounds walleye or other lean fish fillets
   (page 34), ½- to ¾-inch thick, skin on
  Zesty Tomato Sauce (page 141) or
  Lemony White Sauce (page 139)

4 to 6 servings

In fish poacher or large skillet, combine hot water, onion, lemon slices, garlic, salt, allspice, cloves, red pepper and bay leaf. Heat to boiling. Reduce heat. Cover and simmer for 15 minutes.

Lower fish into simmering liquid. Fish should be covered; add additional boiling water as needed. Cover poacher. Simmer until fish flakes easily at thickest part, 5 to 8 minutes. Remove from liquid. Prepare Zesty Tomato Sauce or Lemony White Sauce as directed. Spoon over fish.

Broiled Tarragon Fillets

1½ pounds walleye or other lean fish fillets
    (page 34), about ½-inch thick, skin removed
½ cup margarine or butter
2 tablespoons snipped fresh parsley
2 teaspoons fresh lemon juice
1½ teaspoons dried tarragon leaves
¼ teaspoon salt

4 to 6 servings

Set oven to broil and/or 550°. Grease broiler pan. Cut fish into serving-size pieces. Set aside. In 1-quart saucepan, melt margarine over medium heat. Stir in parsley, lemon juice, tarragon and salt.

Place fish on broiler pan. Baste with margarine. Broil 3 to 4 inches from heat for 3 minutes; turn. Baste with remaining margarine. Broil until fish flakes easily at thickest part, 2 to 3 minutes. Drizzle with remaining margarine before serving.

Northern Pike With Swiss Cheese Sauce

2 tablespoons margarine or butter
2 tablespoons all-purpose flour
½ teaspoon salt
    Dash ground nutmeg
1 cup milk
1 tablespoon sherry, optional
1 cup shredded Swiss cheese
1½ pounds northern pike or other lean
    fish fillets (page 34), about ½-inch thick
½ teaspoon celery salt
⅛ teaspoon pepper
3 tablespoons margarine or butter
½ cup fine dry bread crumbs
1 green pepper

4 to 6 servings

Heat oven to 325°. Grease 13 × 9-inch baking pan. In 1-quart saucepan, melt 2 tablespoons margarine over medium heat. Stir in flour, salt and nutmeg. Blend in milk and sherry. Cook over medium heat, stirring constantly, until thickened and bubbly, about 4 minutes. Stir in cheese until melted. Remove from heat; set aside.

Cut fish into serving-size pieces. Place in prepared pan. Combine celery salt and pepper; sprinkle on fish. Pour cheese sauce over fish.

In small saucepan or skillet, melt 3 tablespoons margarine. Stir in bread crumbs until coated. Sprinkle over fish. Core and seed green pepper; slice into thin rings and place on fish. Bake until fish flakes easily at thickest part, 20 to 25 minutes.

Italian Fish ↑

1½ pounds northern pike or other lean fish
    fillets (page 34), about ½-inch thick, skin
    removed
1 jar (16 ounces) spaghetti sauce
2 tablespoons snipped fresh parsley
½ teaspoon dried basil leaves
¼ teaspoon dried oregano leaves
⅛ teaspoon pepper
1 cup shredded mozzarella cheese

4 to 6 servings

Heat oven to 350°. Cut fish into serving-size pieces. Arrange in 13 × 9-inch baking pan. Pour spaghetti sauce over fish. Sprinkle with parsley, basil, oregano and pepper. Top with cheese. Bake until fish flakes easily at thickest part, 20 to 25 minutes.

Fish Pinwheels

½ cup chopped fresh mushrooms
2 tablespoons finely chopped celery
2 tablespoons finely chopped onion
2 tablespoons margarine or butter
½ cup herb-seasoned stuffing mix
2 tablespoons hot water
½ teaspoon salt
⅛ teaspoon pepper
⅛ teaspoon ground sage
4 northern pike or other lean fish fillets
   (page 34), about ¼-inch thick,
   12 to 15 inches long, skin removed
1 tablespoon margarine or butter, melted
  Mushroom Sauce (page 142)

4 servings

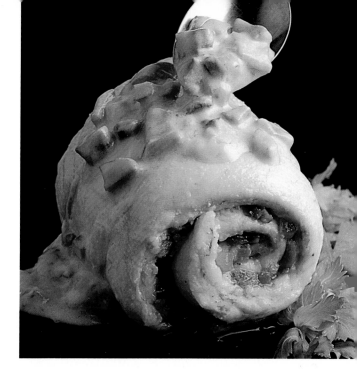

How to Prepare Fish Pinwheels

HEAT oven to 375°. Grease 8 × 4-inch loaf pan. In small skillet, cook and stir mushrooms, celery and onion in 2 tablespoons margarine over medium heat until tender, about 4 minutes.

REMOVE skillet from heat. Add herb-seasoned stuffing mix, hot water, salt, pepper and sage to vegetables. Stir until mixture is moistened.

SPREAD one-fourth of the stuffing mixture evenly on each fillet, pressing lightly. Roll up fillets, starting with narrow ends.

PLACE rolls upright in prepared pan, arranging in staggered pattern. Brush with 1 tablespoon melted margarine. Cover pan with foil.

BAKE until fish in center of roll flakes easily, 30 to 35 minutes. Prepare Mushroom Sauce as directed and serve with fish.

117

Trout Kabobs

1 large green pepper
1 quart water
4 small onions (about ½ pound)
2 pounds trout or other oily fish fillets or
    steaks (page 34), about ¾-inch
    thick, skin removed
16 French bread cubes, 1½ × 1½-inch
1 cup margarine or butter
¾ teaspoon garlic salt
4 metal skewers, 16 inches long
4 lemon wedges

4 servings

How to Prepare Trout Kabobs

CORE and seed green pepper; cut in half. In 3-quart saucepan, heat water to boiling. Add green peppers and onions; cover. Cook over high heat for 4 minutes. Drain. Rinse under cold running water; drain.

CUT onions in half. Cut green pepper into 1-inch pieces. Cut fish into 1-inch chunks. Alternately thread two onion halves, one-fourth of the green pepper pieces, one-fourth of the fish and four bread cubes on each skewer.

PLACE kabobs on lightly greased broiler pan. Set oven to broil and/or 550°. In 1-quart saucepan, heat margarine and garlic salt over medium heat until margarine is melted. Brush on fish, bread and vegetables.

BROIL kabobs 8 to 9 inches from heat, turning and brushing with margarine four times, until fish flakes easily at thickest part, about 8 minutes. Serve kabobs with lemon wedges.

Panfish Stir-Fry

1 pound panfish or other lean fish fillets
    (page 34), ¼- to ½-inch thick, skin on
1 teaspoon cornstarch
2 tablespoons vegetable oil
¼ cup teriyaki sauce
1 tablespoon fresh lemon juice
¼ teaspoon salt
¼ teaspoon garlic powder
⅛ teaspoon pepper
1 pound fresh broccoli
¼ cup vegetable oil
½ cup thinly sliced green onion
1 cup thinly sliced carrot
1 cup sliced fresh mushrooms

                             4 to 6 servings

Cut fillets into 1-inch diagonal strips. In medium bowl, toss fish strips with cornstarch until coated. Add 2 tablespoons vegetable oil, the teriyaki sauce, lemon juice, salt, garlic powder and pepper. Cover and refrigerate at least 30 minutes.

Cut broccoli into flowerets; cut stems into thin slices. In 10-inch skillet, heat ¼ cup vegetable oil. Add broccoli, green onion and carrot, stirring to coat with oil. Cook and stir over medium heat until vegetables are tender-crisp, about 3 minutes.

Stir in fish and marinade; add mushrooms. Cook and stir over medium-high heat until fish flakes easily at thickest part, 4 to 6 minutes.

Variation: Substitute 1 cup thinly sliced celery for the carrot.

Poor Man's Lobster

2½ cups hot water
½ cup white wine
1 small onion, sliced
4 lemon slices
1 teaspoon salt
⅛ teaspoon whole peppercorns
1 small bay leaf
1½ pounds northern pike fillets, about ¾-inch
    thick, skin removed

                             4 to 6 servings

In 10-inch skillet, combine water, white wine, onion, lemon slices, salt, peppercorns and bay leaf. Heat to boiling. Reduce heat. Cover and simmer for 15 minutes.

Cut fish into 1½-inch chunks; add to liquid. Cover and cook over medium heat, occasionally stirring gently until fish flakes easily at thickest part, about 7 minutes. Serve with melted butter and fresh lemon wedges, if desired.

Trout Newburg ↑

1 quart water
1 small onion, sliced
1 lemon slice
1 small bay leaf
⅛ teaspoon whole peppercorns
1 pound trout or other oily fish fillets
    (page 34), ½- to 1-inch thick
1 cup sliced fresh mushrooms
¼ cup margarine or butter
2 tablespoons all-purpose flour
¾ teaspoon salt
1½ cups half-and-half
¾ cup milk
¼ cup sherry
¼ teaspoon paprika
⅛ teaspoon cayenne
3 egg yolks, beaten
8 baked patty shells or 8 pieces toast,
    cut into triangles

                                 4 servings

In fish poacher or 10-inch skillet, combine water, onion, lemon slice, bay leaf and peppercorns. Heat to boiling. Reduce heat. Cover and simmer for 15 minutes. Add fish. Simmer until fish flakes easily at thickest part, 5 to 10 minutes. Remove fish with slotted spatula. Cut into bite-size pieces. Set aside. (Liquid can be strained and refrigerated or frozen for use in soups or chowders.)

In 2-quart saucepan, cook and stir mushrooms in margarine over medium heat until tender, about 4 minutes. Stir in flour and salt. Blend in half-and-half, milk, sherry, paprika and cayenne. Cook over medium heat, stirring constantly, until thickened, about 5 minutes.

Stir about ½ cup of hot mixture into beaten egg yolks. Return to hot mixture. Cook over medium heat until thickened, 1 to 2 minutes. Stir in fish. Serve over patty shells or toast points.

Variation: Substitute ⅓ cup white wine for sherry.

119

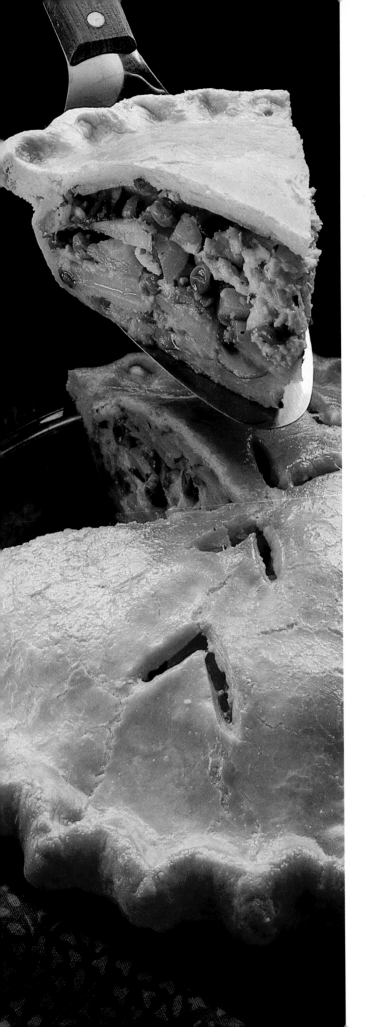

Fish and Vegetable Pie

PASTRY:

  2 cups all-purpose flour
  1 teaspoon salt
⅔ cup shortening
  3 tablespoons margarine or butter,
     room temperature
  5 to 7 tablespoons cold water

FILLING:

  1 tablespoon margarine or butter
  2 tablespoons all-purpose flour
  1 tablespoon snipped fresh parsley
½ teaspoon instant chicken bouillon granules
½ teaspoon salt
⅛ teaspoon pepper
⅛ teaspoon garlic powder
¾ cup milk
  2 medium white potatoes (about 1 pound)
  2 cups flaked cooked trout or other oily fish
     (page 34)
  1 cup sliced fresh mushrooms
½ cup thinly sliced carrot
½ cup frozen peas
  3 tablespoons finely chopped onion
  1 egg
  1 tablespoon water

4 to 6 servings

In medium bowl, combine 2 cups flour and 1 teaspoon salt. Cut shortening and 3 tablespoons margarine into flour until particles resemble coarse crumbs or small peas. Sprinkle with cold water while tossing with fork, until particles are just moist enough to cling together.

Divide pastry in half and shape into two balls. Wrap and refrigerate one ball. On lightly floured board, roll other ball into thin circle at least 2 inches larger than inverted 9-inch pie plate. Fit crust into pie plate, pressing gently against bottom and side. Trim overhang ½ inch from rim. Cover and set aside.

In 1-quart saucepan, melt 1 tablespoon margarine over medium heat. Stir in flour, parsley, bouillon granules, salt, pepper and garlic powder. Blend in milk. Cook, stirring constantly, until thickened and bubbly, about 5 minutes. Set aside.

Heat oven to 375°. Cut potatoes in half lengthwise, then into thin slices. In large bowl, combine potatoes and fish. Add mushrooms, carrot, peas and onion. Stir in sauce.

Fill pastry-lined pie plate with fish mixture. Roll out remaining pastry. Place on filling. Seal and flute edges. Cut several slits in pastry top. Blend egg and 1 tablespoon water. Brush over top before baking. Bake until crust is golden brown, about 1 hour.

Salmon Pie →

CRUST:
  2 cups cooked rice
  3 tablespoons grated Parmesan cheese
  1 egg white

FILLING:
  1 cup flaked cooked salmon or other oily fish
    (page 34)
½ cup half-and-half or milk
  3 eggs, slightly beaten
  1 cup ricotta cheese
¼ cup chopped onion
  2 tablespoons all-purpose flour
  2 tablespoons snipped fresh parsley
⅛ teaspoon salt
⅛ teaspoon pepper
⅛ teaspoon ground oregano
    Paprika, optional

4 to 6 servings

Heat oven to 375°. Grease 9-inch pie plate. In medium bowl, mix rice, Parmesan cheese and egg white. Press into prepared pie plate to form crust. Set aside.

In medium bowl, blend filling ingredients. Pour into rice crust. Sprinkle with paprika. Bake until knife inserted in center comes out clean, 30 to 40 minutes. Let stand 10 minutes before cutting.

Variation: Substitute flaked smoked salmon; omit the salt.

Salmon Loaf With Horseradish Sauce

  2 cups flaked cooked salmon or other oily fish
    (page 34)
  2 eggs, slightly beaten
  1 cup milk
½ cup fine dry bread crumbs
  1 tablespoon snipped fresh parsley
  1 tablespoon sliced green onion
½ teaspoon grated lime peel
½ teaspoon salt
⅛ teaspoon pepper
  3 tablespoons prepared horseradish
  1 tablespoon plus 1 teaspoon soy sauce

4 to 6 servings

Heat oven to 350°. Generously grease 8 × 4-inch loaf pan. In medium bowl, combine all ingredients except horseradish and soy sauce. Spread in prepared pan. Bake until center is firm and loaf is golden brown, 55 to 60 minutes. Loosen edges with spatula and turn out of loaf pan; cut into slices.

In small dish, blend horseradish and soy sauce. Serve with salmon loaf.

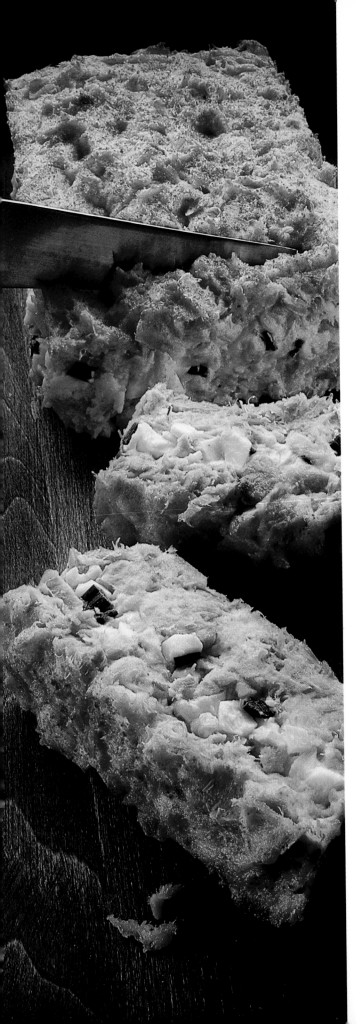

← Layered Salmon Loaf

    2 tablespoons margarine or butter
    2 tablespoons all-purpose flour
  ⅛ teaspoon salt
  ⅛ teaspoon pepper
    1 cup half-and-half
    2 cups flaked cooked salmon or other oily fish
        (page 34)
    1 egg
    2 slices soft bread, crusts removed, and bread
        crumbled (about 1¼ cups)
    2 hard-cooked eggs
    2 tablespoons chopped green onion
    1 teaspoon prepared mustard

4 to 6 servings

Heat oven to 350°. Generously grease 8 × 4-inch loaf pan. In 1-quart saucepan, melt margarine over medium heat. Stir in flour, salt and pepper. Blend in half-and-half. Cook over medium heat, stirring constantly, until thickened and bubbly, about 4 minutes. Remove from heat.

In medium bowl, combine fish, one egg, the crumbled bread and ¾ cup hot white sauce; set aside. Finely chop hard-cooked eggs. In small bowl, combine chopped eggs, onion, remaining sauce and mustard. In prepared pan, layer half the fish mixture, then the egg mixture. Top with remaining fish mixture. Sprinkle top of loaf with paprika, if desired. Bake until center is firm, 45 to 50 minutes.

Easy Northern Pike Loaf

  1½ cups cracker crumbs
    ⅓ cup milk
    2 cups flaked cooked northern pike or other lean
        fish (page 34)
    1 can (10¾ ounces) condensed cream of
        shrimp soup
    2 eggs, slightly beaten
    2 tablespoons finely chopped green onion
  ¼ teaspoon lemon pepper
  ⅛ teaspoon garlic powder

4 to 6 servings

Heat oven to 350°. Generously grease 8 × 4-inch loaf pan. In medium bowl, combine cracker crumbs and milk. Let stand to moisten crumbs, about 5 minutes. Stir in fish, cream of shrimp soup, eggs, green onion, lemon pepper and garlic powder. Spread mixture in prepared pan.

Bake until knife inserted in center comes out clean and loaf is golden brown, 55 to 60 minutes. If desired, serve with Mushroom Sauce, page 142.

Variation: Substitute 1 can (10¾ ounces) condensed clam chowder for the cream of shrimp soup.

Oven-Fried Trout Cakes ↑

1½ cups cold mashed potatoes*
1½ cups flaked cooked trout or other oily fish
   (page 34)
 1 egg, slightly beaten
 2 tablespoons snipped fresh parsley
 2 tablespoons grated onion
 1 teaspoon fresh lemon juice
 ½ teaspoon celery salt
 ⅛ teaspoon pepper
 ¼ cup all-purpose flour
 1 egg
 1 tablespoon milk
 1 cup fine dry bread crumbs
 1 tablespoon snipped fresh parsley
 ½ teaspoon paprika
 6 tablespoons vegetable oil
   Lemon-Parsley Sauce (page 139)

4 servings

In medium bowl, combine mashed potatoes, fish, one beaten egg, 2 tablespoons parsley, the onion, lemon juice, celery salt and pepper. Set aside.

Heat oven to 450°. Sprinkle flour on plate or waxed paper. In shallow dish or pie plate, blend one egg and milk. On another plate or waxed paper, combine crumbs, 1 tablespoon parsley and the paprika.

Drop ⅓ cup of fish mixture into flour. Roll gently to coat. Place in egg mixture. Flatten slightly to form ½-inch thick patty. Turn to coat with egg. Carefully coat with bread crumbs. Repeat with remaining fish mixture. Set aside.

Coat bottom of 13 × 9-inch baking pan with oil. Place pan in oven for 5 minutes to heat oil. Add fish cakes. Bake for 8 minutes; turn. Bake until golden brown, about 7 minutes.

Prepare Lemon-Parsley Sauce as directed. Serve over fish cakes.

*Use leftover mashed potatoes or substitute cooked instant mashed potatoes.

Northern Pike Patties

 2 cups water
 ½ teaspoon salt
 1 medium red potato (about 6 ounces)
 1 pound skinless northern pike or other lean fish
   fillets (page 34)
 1 egg
 1 cup milk
 ½ cup cracker crumbs
 2 tablespoons finely chopped onion
 1 teaspoon Worcestershire sauce
 ½ teaspoon salt
 ¼ teaspoon pepper
 1 cup dry bread crumbs or cornflake crumbs
 2 tablespoons vegetable oil
 1 tablespoon margarine or butter
   Mustard Sauce (page 142)

4 to 6 servings

In 1-quart saucepan, heat water and ½ teaspoon salt to boiling; add potato. Return to boiling. Reduce heat. Cover and simmer until potato is tender, about 20 minutes. Drain. Cool.

Cut fish into 3-inch pieces. Place fish and egg in food processor.* Process, slowly adding milk, until smooth, 1 to 2 minutes. In medium bowl, mix fish, cracker crumbs, onion, Worcestershire sauce, ½ teaspoon salt and the pepper. Peel potato and shred; stir into fish mixture. Refrigerate 30 minutes.

Sprinkle bread crumbs on plate or waxed paper. Form fish mixture into eight ½-inch thick patties. Coat with bread crumbs, pressing lightly. Place on baking sheet or tray.

In 9-inch skillet, heat oil and margarine over medium-high heat. Place four patties in skillet. Fry for 2 minutes; turn. Fry until golden brown, about 2 minutes. Drain on paper towels. Keep warm in 175° oven. Repeat with remaining fish mixture. Prepare Mustard Sauce as directed. Serve with fish patties. If desired, serve patties in hamburger buns with lettuce and tomato slices.

*If using blender, purée half the fish and milk at a time. Proceed as directed.

Stuffed Cabbage Rolls

    2 quarts water
    8 large cabbage leaves*
 ⅓ cup finely chopped celery
 ¼ cup finely chopped onion
    1 tablespoon margarine or butter
    2 cups flaked cooked northern pike or other
       lean fish (page 34)
    1 cup uncooked instant rice
    1 egg, slightly beaten
    2 tablespoons snipped fresh parsley
    1 tablespoon fresh lemon juice
 ½ teaspoon salt
 ¼ teaspoon garlic salt
 ⅛ teaspoon pepper
    4 drops red pepper sauce
SAUCE:
    1 can (15 ounces) tomato sauce
 1½ teaspoons sugar
 ⅛ teaspoon garlic salt
    4 thin lemon slices

                                              4 servings

*To loosen leaves from cabbage head, cut out core.
Place cabbage in bowl; cover with cold water. Let
stand about 10 minutes; remove leaves.

How to Prepare Stuffed Cabbage Rolls

HEAT water to boiling in Dutch oven. Add four cabbage
leaves; cover. Cook over high heat until pliable, about 2
minutes. Remove with slotted spoon to colander. Rinse
under cold running water; drain. Repeat with remaining
four leaves. Set aside.

COOK and stir celery and onion in margarine in small
skillet over medium heat until tender-crisp, about 2 minutes. In medium bowl, mix celery and onion with remaining ingredients except sauce ingredients. Set aside. Heat
oven to 350°.

CUT out hard center rib from each cabbage leaf. Overlap
cut edges of leaves; place about ⅓ cup of fish mixture on
base of each. Fold in sides; roll up to enclose filling. Place
rolls, seam side down, in 9 × 9-inch baking pan.

COMBINE tomato sauce, sugar and ⅛ teaspoon garlic
salt in small bowl or 2-cup measure. Pour over cabbage
rolls. Top with lemon slices. Cover with foil. Bake until
heated, about 35 to 40 minutes.

Smoked Fish and Potato Casserole

    4 medium white potatoes (about 2 pounds)
    1 medium onion, chopped
1½ cups flaked smoked fish
    3 tablespoons margarine or butter
    2 tablespoons snipped fresh parsley
    ¼ teaspoon pepper
    ⅓ cup water

4 to 6 servings

Heat oven to 350°. Grease 2-quart casserole. Cut potatoes into thin slices. Layer half each of the potato slices, onion, fish, margarine, parsley and pepper in casserole. Repeat layers. Pour water over layers in casserole; cover. Bake until potatoes are tender, about 1¼ hours. Serve with margarine and snipped fresh parsley, if desired.

Trout and Corn Bake

    1 medium green pepper
    1 tablespoon margarine or butter
    4 slices bacon, cut up
1½ cups flaked cooked trout or other oily fish
        (page 34)
    1 package (10 ounces) frozen whole kernel corn
    1 cup coarse cracker crumbs
    1 can (13 ounces) evaporated milk
    3 tablespoons margarine or butter, melted
    2 tablespoons grated onion
    2 tablespoons snipped fresh parsley
    ½ teaspoon celery salt
    ⅛ teaspoon pepper
    ⅓ cup grated Parmesan cheese
    ⅛ teaspoon paprika

4 to 6 servings

Heat oven to 350°. Grease 9×9-inch baking pan. Core and seed green pepper. Cut two thin rings and set aside. Chop remaining green pepper. In 9-inch skillet, cook and stir chopped green pepper in 1 tablespoon margarine over medium heat until tender-crisp, about 4 minutes. Remove to medium bowl. Set aside.

In 9-inch skillet, cook and stir bacon over medium-high heat until crisp. Remove bacon with slotted spoon. Add bacon and 1 tablespoon bacon fat to green pepper. Discard remaining bacon fat. Stir in fish, corn, cracker crumbs, evaporated milk, melted margarine, onion, parsley, celery salt and pepper. Spread fish mixture in prepared pan.

In small dish, mix Parmesan cheese and paprika. Sprinkle over fish. Top with reserved green pepper rings. Bake until knife inserted in center comes out clean, 40 to 45 minutes. Let stand 5 minutes. Cut into squares to serve.

Creamy Northern Pike Casserole

1 cup thinly sliced celery
1 tablespoon margarine or butter
2 cups flaked cooked northern pike or other lean fish (page 34)
1 can (10¾ ounces) condensed cream of shrimp soup
1 cup frozen green beans
1 can (5.3 ounces) evaporated milk
1 can (4 ounces) sliced mushrooms, drained
1 can (3 ounces) French-fried onion rings, crushed
⅛ teaspoon pepper

4 to 6 servings

Heat oven to 350°. In small skillet, cook and stir celery in margarine over medium heat until tender, about 6 minutes. Set aside.

In 2-quart casserole, mix fish, cream of shrimp soup, green beans, milk, mushrooms, ½ cup of the crushed onion rings and the pepper. Stir in celery.

Bake for 30 minutes. Top with remaining onion rings. Bake until hot and bubbly, 15 to 20 minutes.

Cheesy Bass and Rice Casserole

2 cups flaked cooked bass or other lean fish (page 34)
⅔ cup uncooked long-grain rice
⅔ cup shredded Cheddar cheese
⅓ cup sliced celery
⅓ cup chopped green pepper
¼ cup chopped onion
1 can (10¾ ounces) condensed chicken broth
1 can (4 ounces) mushroom pieces, drained
1 jar (2 ounces) sliced pimiento, drained
1 tablespoon Worcestershire sauce
¼ teaspoon salt
⅛ teaspoon pepper
½ cup herb-seasoned croutons
⅓ cup shredded Cheddar cheese

6 servings

Heat oven to 350°. In 1½-quart casserole, mix all ingredients except croutons and ⅓ cup cheese. Cover. Bake until rice is tender, 50 to 55 minutes. Stir. Sprinkle with croutons and ⅓ cup cheese. Bake, uncovered, until cheese melts, about 5 minutes.

Panfish Asparagus Biscuit Bake ↑

1 cup diced carrot
1 small onion, chopped
2 tablespoons margarine or butter
2 cups flaked cooked panfish or other lean fish
    (page 34)
1 can (10¾ ounces) condensed cream of
    mushroom soup
1 package (10 ounces) frozen asparagus
    cuts, thawed
¼ cup milk
2 teaspoons fresh lemon juice
¼ teaspoon salt
⅛ teaspoon pepper
1 cup buttermilk baking mix
⅓ cup milk
1 teaspoon dried parsley flakes
    Dash paprika

4 to 6 servings

Heat oven to 375°. In 9-inch skillet, cook and stir carrot and onion in margarine over medium heat until tender, about 11 minutes. Remove to 1½-quart casserole. Stir in fish, cream of mushroom soup, asparagus cuts, ¼ cup milk, the lemon juice, salt and pepper. Set aside.

In small bowl, combine baking mix, ⅓ cup milk, the parsley flakes and paprika. Mix with fork. Drop eight mounds of dough on fish mixture in casserole.

Bake until biscuits are golden brown and casserole is bubbly, about 35 minutes. Brush biscuits with melted margarine before serving, if desired.

Spicy Trout and Rice Casserole

1 medium zucchini (about ¼ pound)
½ cup chopped celery
⅓ cup chopped onion
1 clove garlic, minced
2 tablespoons vegetable oil
1 can (8 ounces) tomato sauce
½ cup water
1 tablespoon fresh lemon juice
1 teaspoon sugar
½ teaspoon chili powder
¼ teaspoon salt
⅛ teaspoon cayenne
2 cups flaked cooked trout or other oily fish
    (page 34)
½ cup uncooked instant rice
⅓ cup shredded Cheddar cheese
⅓ cup shredded Monterey Jack cheese
    Paprika

4 to 6 servings

Heat oven to 350°. Cut zucchini lengthwise into fourths, then into ¼-inch thick slices. In 9-inch skillet, cook and stir zucchini, celery, onion and garlic in oil over medium heat until tender, about 7 minutes. Stir in tomato sauce, water, lemon juice, sugar, chili powder, salt and cayenne. Heat to boiling. Reduce heat. Cover and simmer for 10 minutes.

Pour into 1-quart casserole. Stir in fish and rice. Sprinkle Cheddar and Monterey Jack cheese on top. Sprinkle with paprika. Bake until casserole is heated and rice is tender, about 30 minutes.

Fish Melt ↑

1½ cups flaked cooked northern pike or other
    lean fish (page 34)
¼ cup finely chopped cucumber
2 tablespoons chopped radish
1 tablespoon mayonnaise or salad dressing
1 tablespoon dairy sour cream
½ teaspoon salt
⅛ teaspoon pepper
4 large thin tomato slices
4 to 8 slices whole wheat bread, toasted
4 slices American cheese

2 to 4 servings

Set oven to broil and/or 550°. In small bowl, mix
fish, cucumber, radish, mayonnaise, sour cream,
salt and pepper. Place one tomato slice on each of
four toasted bread slices. Spread fish mixture over
tomatoes; spread to edges of bread. Top each piece
with one piece of cheese. Place sandwiches on baking sheet. Broil 2 to 3 inches from heat until cheese
melts, about 2 minutes. Top each sandwich with
another piece of toast, if desired.

Baked Salmon Sandwiches

1½ cups flaked cooked salmon or other oily fish
    (page 34)
¼ cup mayonnaise or salad dressing
2 tablespoons finely chopped onion
2 tablespoons sliced stuffed green olives
1 tablespoon sweet pickle relish
2 teaspoons lime juice, optional
½ teaspoon salt
⅛ teaspoon pepper
4 hamburger buns
½ cup shredded Monterey Jack cheese

2 to 4 servings

Heat oven to 400°. In small bowl, mix fish, mayonnaise, onion, green olives, pickle relish, lime juice,
salt and pepper. Spread fish mixture on buns. Top
with cheese. Replace tops. Wrap sandwiches in foil.
Bake until fish mixture is hot and cheese is melted,
about 15 minutes.

Smoked Fish Omelet

  3 eggs
  2 tablespoons milk
⅛ teaspoon pepper
  1 tablespoon margarine or butter
½ cup flaked smoked fish
¼ cup shredded Cheddar or Swiss cheese

2 servings

In small bowl, blend eggs, milk and pepper. In 10-inch skillet, melt margarine over medium heat. Pour eggs into skillet. Cook until eggs are set, about 5 minutes. Sprinkle fish and cheese over one half of the omelet. With spatula, carefully fold other half over filling. Cook until cheese melts, 1 to 2 minutes.

Egg Foo Yung

¾ cup water
  1 teaspoon instant chicken bouillon granules
  1 tablespoon plus 1 teaspoon soy sauce
  2 teaspoons sugar
  1 tablespoon cornstarch
  2 tablespoons cold water
  6 eggs
1½ cups flaked cooked northern pike or other
      lean fish (page 34)
  1 can (16 ounces) bean sprouts, drained
  1 can (4½ ounces) small shrimp,
      rinsed and drained
  1 can (4 ounces) sliced mushrooms, drained
  2 tablespoons thinly sliced green onion
  1 teaspoon soy sauce
⅛ teaspoon pepper
  1 tablespoon margarine or butter

4 to 6 servings

In 1-quart saucepan, combine ¾ cup water, bouillon granules, 1 tablespoon plus 1 teaspoon soy sauce and the sugar. Heat to boiling. In small dish, blend cornstarch into 2 tablespoons cold water. Stir into boiling mixture. Return to boiling. Cook, stirring constantly, until thickened and translucent, about 2 minutes. Keep warm over very low heat.

In medium bowl, beat eggs well. Stir in fish, bean sprouts, shrimp, mushrooms, green onion, 1 teaspoon soy sauce and the pepper. In 9-inch skillet, melt margarine over medium heat. Form four patties by dropping ⅓ cup of egg mixture for each patty into skillet. Cook over medium heat for 3 minutes; turn. Cook until set, 2 to 3 minutes. Repeat with remaining egg mixture. Keep warm in 175° oven. Serve warm sauce over patties.

Mushroom Fish Omelet ↑

  1 cup sliced fresh mushrooms
  2 tablespoons chopped green pepper
  2 tablespoons chopped onion
  2 tablespoons margarine or butter
  3 eggs
  2 tablespoons milk
⅛ teaspoon pepper
  1 tablespoon margarine or butter
½ cup flaked smoked fish

2 servings

In 10-inch skillet, cook and stir mushrooms, green pepper and onion in 2 tablespoons margarine over medium heat until tender, about 5 minutes. Remove to small dish; set aside.

In small bowl, blend eggs, milk and pepper. In 10-inch skillet, melt 1 tablespoon margarine over medium heat. Pour eggs into skillet. Cook until eggs are set, about 5 minutes.

Spoon vegetables and fish over one half of the omelet. With spatula, carefully fold other half of omelet over filling. Cook until hot, about 1 minute.

129

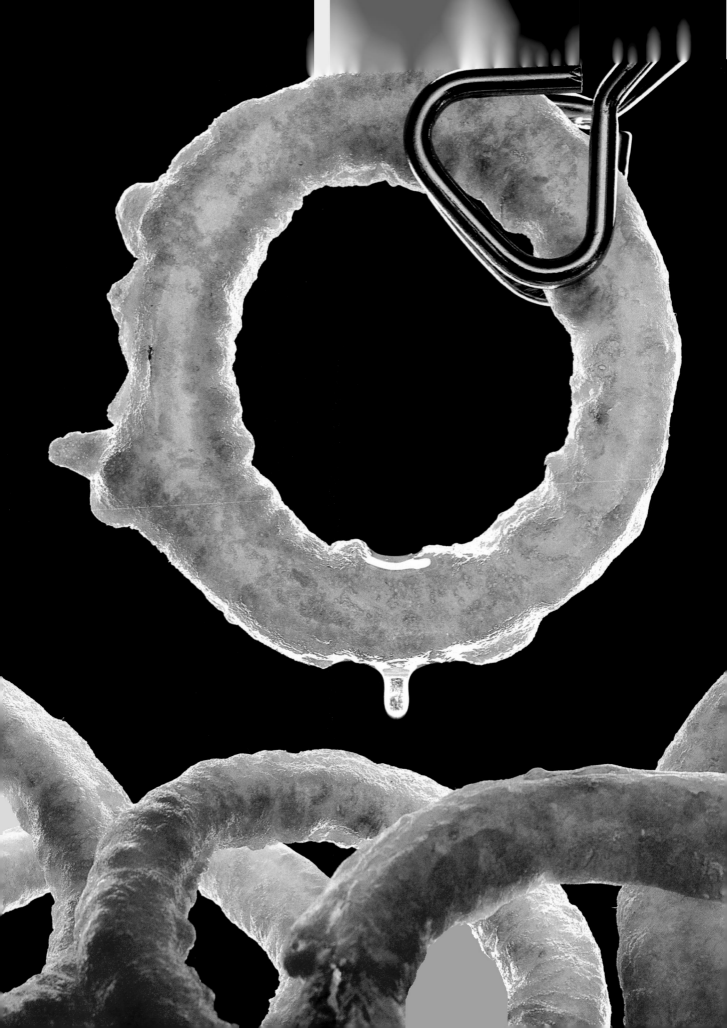

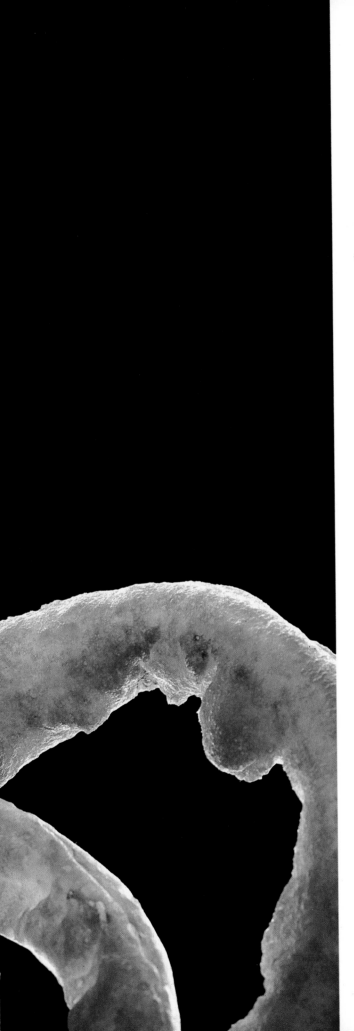

Fish Complements

Some dishes such as coleslaw, French fries and hush puppies just naturally go with fish. Other dishes, especially vegetables and salads, taste good and add color and appeal to the fish. Both types of dishes are included in this section.

← Beer Batter Onion Rings

1 cup all-purpose flour
1 cup beer
½ teaspoon salt
1 large onion (about 1 pound)
2 cups milk
  Vegetable oil
½ cup all-purpose flour

35 to 40 onion rings

In medium bowl, beat 1 cup flour, the beer and salt with fork. Cover and refrigerate batter 3 hours. Cut onion into ½-inch slices and separate into rings. Place onion rings in shallow dish. Pour milk over onions. Cover with plastic wrap. Refrigerate 3 hours, turning rings over one or two times.

In deep-fat fryer or saucepan, heat oil (2 to 3 inches) to 375°. Place ½ cup flour in paper or plastic bag. Shake onions in flour until coated, then dip in batter. Fry a few rings at a time, turning over one or two times, until golden brown, 1½ to 2 minutes. Drain on paper towels. Keep warm in 175° oven.

Corn Muffins

1 cup yellow cornmeal
1 cup all-purpose flour
2 tablespoons sugar
1 tablespoon baking powder
½ teaspoon salt
1 cup milk
1 egg
3 tablespoons vegetable oil
2 tablespoons chopped green pepper, optional
2 tablespoons chopped onion, optional

8 × 8-inch pan or 12 muffins

Heat oven to 425°. Grease 8 × 8-inch baking pan or line 12 muffin cups with paper liners. In medium bowl, combine cornmeal, flour, sugar, baking powder and salt. Beat in remaining ingredients until smooth. Pour batter into prepared pan or fill muffin cups one-half full. Bake until light golden brown, about 25 minutes.

Buttermilk Batter Onion Rings

1 large onion (about 1 pound)
1 cup buttermilk pancake mix
1 cup buttermilk
1 egg
  Vegetable oil

35 to 40 onion rings

Cut onion into ½-inch slices and separate into rings. Spread pancake mix on waxed paper or place in paper bag. In medium bowl, beat buttermilk and egg with fork until smooth. Dip a few onion rings at a time into buttermilk mixture, then coat thoroughly with pancake mix. Let stand on wire rack until dry, 1½ to 2 hours.

In deep-fat fryer or saucepan, heat oil (2 to 3 inches) to 375°. Fry a few rings at a time, turning over one or two times, until golden brown, 1½ to 2 minutes. Drain on paper towels. Keep warm in 175° oven.

French Fries

  Vegetable oil
2 medium baking potatoes (about 1 pound)
  Salt

4 to 6 servings

In deep-fat fryer or saucepan, heat oil (2 to 3 inches) to 375°. Cut potatoes lengthwise into ½-inch thick slices, then into ¼-inch strips. Rinse and pat dry.

Fry a few pieces at a time, stirring one or two times, until crisp and deep golden brown, 8 to 10 minutes. Drain on paper towels. Sprinkle with salt. Keep warm in 175° oven.

Rice Ring

¼ cup finely chopped celery
¼ cup chopped filberts, almonds or pecans
2 tablespoons chopped green onion
3 tablespoons margarine or butter
3 cups water
1½ cups uncooked long-grain brown rice
1 teaspoon salt
⅛ teaspoon pepper

6 servings

In small saucepan or skillet, cook and stir celery, filberts and green onion in margarine over medium heat until vegetables are tender. In 2-quart saucepan, combine remaining ingredients. Stir in vegetables and filberts. Heat to boiling. Reduce heat. Cover tightly and simmer until moisture is absorbed, about 50 minutes. Fluff with fork. Spoon rice into 4-cup mold, pressing lightly. Unmold onto warm serving plate.

Hush Puppies ↑

  Vegetable oil
1 cup yellow cornmeal
⅓ cup all-purpose flour
1 teaspoon sugar
1 teaspoon baking powder
⅛ teaspoon salt
⅛ teaspoon cayenne, optional
1 egg
¼ cup chopped onion
1 can (8 ounces) cream-style corn
2 tablespoons buttermilk

4 to 6 servings

In deep-fat fryer or saucepan, heat oil (2 to 3 inches) to 375°. Mix cornmeal, flour, sugar, baking powder, salt and cayenne. Stir in remaining ingredients until just combined. Drop batter by tablespoonfuls into hot oil. Fry a few at a time, turning over one or two times, until dark golden brown, 4 to 5 minutes. Drain on paper towels. Keep warm in 175° oven.

Vegetables With Crumb Topping

Vegetable oil
½ cup all-purpose flour
¼ teaspoon salt
⅛ teaspoon pepper
2 eggs
1 teaspoon milk
1 cup fine dry bread crumbs

RECIPE COATS ONE OF THE FOLLOWING:
1 large onion (about 1 pound), cut into ½-inch
   slices and separated into rings, 35 to 40 pieces
3 medium green peppers, seeded and cut into
   ½-inch rings, about 18 pieces
3 small zucchini (about 1 pound), cut in half
   lengthwise, seeded and cut into
   2½ × ½-inch strips, about 50 pieces
½ pound cheese (Colby, Swiss or Cheddar),
   cut into ¾-inch pieces, about 40 pieces

4 to 6 servings

In deep-fat fryer or saucepan, heat oil (2 to 3 inches) to 375°. In paper or plastic bag, mix flour, salt and pepper. Rinse vegetables (not cheese) with water; do not dry. Shake about one-third of vegetables or cheese in bag until coated with flour. Remove; set aside. Repeat with remaining vegetables or cheese.

In small bowl, beat eggs and milk. Dip flour-coated vegetables in egg, then coat with crumbs. Fry a few pieces at a time, turning over one or two times, until deep golden brown, 1 to 1½ minutes. Drain on paper towels. Keep warm in 175° oven.

Almond Crumb-Baked Tomatoes

¼ cup mayonnaise or salad dressing
2 tablespoons dairy sour cream
⅛ to ¼ teaspoon dried dillweed
⅓ cup margarine or butter
½ cup dry seasoned bread crumbs
¼ cup grated Parmesan cheese
¼ cup sliced almonds, chopped
3 medium tomatoes, cut in half

6 servings

In small bowl, mix mayonnaise, sour cream and dillweed. Cover and refrigerate.

Heat oven to 375°. In small saucepan, melt margarine over medium heat. Remove from heat. Stir in bread crumbs, Parmesan cheese and almonds. Place tomato halves, cut side up, on broiler pan. Sprinkle crumb mixture equally on tomato halves. Gently press mixture on top of tomatoes. Bake until base of tomatoes can be pierced easily with fork and crumbs are light brown, 20 to 25 minutes. Serve with mayonnaise topping.

Vegetable Kabobs With Lemon Butter →

4 small red potatoes (1½- to 2-inch diameter)
2 small onions
1 medium zucchini or yellow summer squash
2 medium green peppers
8 cherry tomatoes
8 lemon wedges
4 metal skewers, 16 inches long
⅓ cup margarine or butter
2 tablespoons grated Parmesan cheese
½ teaspoon lemon pepper
⅛ teaspoon garlic powder

4 kabobs

Remove thin strip of peel from around center of each potato. In 2-quart saucepan, place potatoes and onions. Cover with cold water. Heat over low heat to boiling. Simmer until potatoes can just be pierced with fork, 5 to 8 minutes. Drain. Immediately plunge into cold water to cool.

Cut each onion into four wedges. Cut zucchini into eight chunks. Cut each green pepper into eight cubes. Alternately thread two zucchini chunks, two cherry tomatoes, four green pepper cubes, one potato, two onion wedges and two lemon wedges on each skewer. Place kabobs on broiler pan.

In small saucepan, melt margarine over medium heat. Stir in remaining ingredients. Brush evenly over each kabob. Set oven to broil and/or 550°. Broil 6 inches from heat, turning kabobs over after half the time, until potatoes are fork tender and other vegetables are light brown, 16 to 20 minutes.

← Orange-Broccoli Stir-Fry

¾ pound fresh broccoli
2 tablespoons hot water
1 teaspoon instant chicken bouillon granules
1 tablespoon sesame seed
1 small clove garlic, cut in half
2 tablespoons vegetable oil
1 tablespoon grated orange peel
¼ teaspoon ground ginger
1 can (8 ounces) sliced water chestnuts, drained
1 cup fresh or drained canned bean sprouts
1 jar (2 ounces) chopped pimiento, drained

4 to 6 servings

Separate broccoli into flowerets. Cut stems into ¼-inch slices. Set aside. Mix hot water and bouillon granules. Set aside. In 10-inch skillet, cook and stir sesame seed and garlic in oil over medium heat for 3 minutes. Add orange peel. Cook and stir until sesame seed is golden brown. Remove garlic. Stir in ginger. Add broccoli and remaining ingredients. Cook and stir over medium heat until broccoli is tender, about 7 minutes.

Carrot and Celery Stir-Fry

3 stalks celery
2 large carrots
2 tablespoons slivered almonds
¼ teaspoon grated lemon peel
¼ cup margarine or butter
1 tablespoon white wine

4 servings

Cut celery diagonally into thin slices. Cut carrots diagonally into thin slices. In 9-inch skillet, cook and stir almonds and lemon peel in margarine over medium heat until almonds are light brown. Stir in celery, carrots and wine. Cook and stir over medium heat until carrots and celery are tender-crisp, about 6 minutes.

Frozen Fruit Salad

½ cup flaked coconut
1 package (3 ounces) cream cheese, softened
1 container (12 ounces) prepared frozen whipped dessert topping, thawed
1 can (15¼ ounces) crushed pineapple, drained
1 can (11 ounces) mandarin orange segments, drained
1 cup chopped pecans
½ cup chopped maraschino cherries

8 to 9 servings

Set oven to broil and/or 550°. Spread coconut evenly on baking sheet. Broil 4 inches from heat until golden brown, about 1 minute. Set aside.

In large bowl, place cream cheese. Gradually blend in whipped topping at medium speed of electric mixer. Mix in remaining ingredients except coconut. Spread mixture in 8 × 8-inch baking pan. Sprinkle with toasted coconut. Cover and freeze until firm, at least 2 hours. Cut into squares.

Potato Salad

1 quart water
1 teaspoon salt
4 medium red potatoes (about 2 pounds)
3 hard-cooked eggs
½ cup chopped onion
¼ cup shredded carrot
1 stalk celery with leaves, chopped
½ teaspoon salt
⅛ teaspoon pepper
1 cup mayonnaise or salad dressing
1 teaspoon prepared mustard
  Paprika

4 to 6 servings

In 3-quart saucepan, heat water and 1 teaspoon salt to boiling. Add potatoes. Return to boiling. Reduce heat. Cover and simmer until tender, 25 to 35 minutes. Cool. Peel and cut into ¾-inch cubes.

Chop two eggs. Cut remaining egg into slices. In medium bowl, combine potato cubes, chopped eggs, onion, carrot, celery, ½ teaspoon salt and the pepper. Stir in mayonnaise and mustard until just combined. Garnish with sliced egg; sprinkle with paprika. Cover and refrigerate 2 to 3 hours.

Fresh Fruit Salad ↑

½ cup apple jelly
½ cup rosé wine
¼ cup sugar
2 oranges, peeled and sectioned
1 grapefruit, peeled and sectioned
1 apple, cored and thinly sliced
1 pear, cored and thinly sliced

4 to 6 servings

In small saucepan, cook and stir jelly, wine and sugar over medium heat until jelly dissolves and mixture boils. Cool glaze until lukewarm.

In medium bowl, combine fruits. Pour glaze over fruit, tossing to coat. Cover and refrigerate until chilled, 2 to 3 hours. Drain before serving. Garnish with dairy sour cream, if desired.

Lemony Cucumber and Apple Mold →

    1 package (6 ounces) lemon gelatin
    2 cups boiling water
1½ cups cold water
    1 cup chopped, seeded, peeled cucumber
    1 cup cored, chopped apple
    ¼ cup chopped green onion
    8 to 10 very thin slices cucumber, optional

6 to 8 servings

Dissolve gelatin in boiling water. Add cold water. Refrigerate 1 to 1½ hours until soft-set, stirring one or two times. Stir in chopped cucumber, apple and green onion. In bottom of 6-cup mold, arrange cucumber slices. Spoon gelatin mixture evenly over slices. Refrigerate until firm. Unmold onto serving plate lined with lettuce or watercress.

Creamy Coleslaw

    4 cups shredded cabbage
    ⅓ cup shredded carrot
    ¼ cup chopped green pepper

DRESSING:
    ½ cup mayonnaise or salad dressing
    3 tablespoons dairy sour cream
    1 tablespoon plus 2 teaspoons cider vinegar
    1 teaspoon sugar
    ½ teaspoon salt
    ½ teaspoon celery seed, optional
    ⅛ teaspoon pepper

6 to 8 servings

In large bowl, combine cabbage, carrot and green pepper. In small bowl, blend all dressing ingredients. Add to cabbage mixture, tossing gently to coat. Cover and refrigerate at least 3 hours.

Cabbage Vinaigrette

    4 cups shredded cabbage
    ⅓ cup chopped green pepper
    ⅓ cup snipped fresh parsley
    ¼ cup finely chopped onion
    ¼ cup vinegar
    1 tablespoon vegetable oil
    2 teaspoons sugar
    ½ teaspoon dry mustard
    ¼ teaspoon celery seed
    ¼ teaspoon salt

6 to 8 servings

In medium bowl, combine cabbage, green pepper, parsley and onion. In small bowl, mix vinegar, oil, sugar, mustard, celery seed and salt; add to cabbage, tossing gently to coat. Cover and refrigerate 3 to 4 hours.

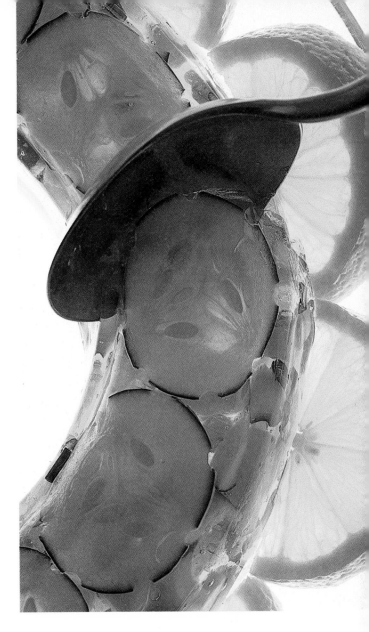

Tomato-Cucumber Salad

    1 medium cucumber, peeled, seeded and chopped
    1 large tomato, seeded and finely chopped
    ½ cup crumbled corn bread*
    ¼ cup chopped green onion
    ¼ cup chopped green pepper
    ¼ cup snipped fresh parsley
    ¼ cup vegetable oil
    1 tablespoon vinegar
    1 teaspoon sugar
    ⅛ teaspoon salt
       Dash pepper

4 to 6 servings

In medium bowl, combine cucumber, tomato, corn bread, green onion, green pepper and parsley. In small bowl, mix remaining ingredients. Add dressing to vegetable mixture, tossing gently to coat. Serve immediately.

*Or use one corn muffin, crumbled, page 131.

Sauces

A good sauce enhances the taste of fish without covering the natural flavor. It can be simple or complex, but it adds a unique flavor to the cooked fish. For extra tang, substitute fish stock for water, wine or half of the milk or cream in the sauce recipe.

← Lemon-Parsley Sauce

  1 tablespoon cornstarch
¾ cup cold water
  1 tablespoon grated lemon peel
  1 teaspoon fresh lemon juice
½ teaspoon sugar
¼ teaspoon salt
  1 tablespoon snipped fresh parsley
  1 tablespoon margarine or butter

¾ cup sauce

In small saucepan, gradually blend cornstarch into water. Stir in lemon peel, lemon juice, sugar and salt. Cook over medium heat, stirring constantly, until thickened, about 3 minutes. Add parsley and margarine, stirring until margarine is melted.

Lemony White Sauce

2 tablespoons margarine or butter
2 tablespoons all-purpose flour
⅛ teaspoon salt
⅛ teaspoon white pepper
  1 cup half-and-half
  1 tablespoon snipped fresh parsley
¼ teaspoon grated lemon peel

1 cup sauce

In small saucepan, melt margarine over medium heat. Stir in flour, salt and white pepper. Blend in half-and-half, parsley and lemon peel. Cook over medium heat, stirring constantly, until thickened, about 4 minutes.

Basic Tartar Sauce

½ cup mayonnaise or salad dressing
  2 tablespoons chopped sweet pickle relish
  2 tablespoons dairy sour cream
  2 tablespoons fresh lime or lemon juice
  2 teaspoons finely chopped onion
⅛ teaspoon salt
    Dash curry powder, optional

¾ cup sauce

In small bowl, mix all ingredients. Chill at least 30 minutes to blend flavors.

NOTE: Recipe can be doubled.

Flavored Softened Butters ↑

CITRUS BUTTER *(pictured)*:
 6 tablespoons margarine or butter, softened
 ¼ teaspoon grated orange, lemon or lime peel

LEMON-PARSLEY BUTTER:
 6 tablespoons margarine or butter, softened
 1 tablespoon snipped fresh parsley
 ¼ teaspoon fresh lemon juice

DILL BUTTER:
 6 tablespoons margarine or butter, softened
 ⅛ teaspoon dried dillweed

⅓ cup butter each

In small bowl, combine softened margarine and remaining ingredients.

Almondine Butter

 1 tablespoon margarine or butter
 ¼ cup sliced almonds
 5 tablespoons margarine or butter
 1 tablespoon fresh lemon juice
   Dash cayenne

½ cup butter

In small skillet, melt 1 tablespoon margarine over medium heat. Add almonds. Cook and stir over medium heat until almonds are light brown, about 4 minutes. Stir in 5 tablespoons margarine, the lemon juice and cayenne. Cook over medium heat, stirring constantly, until margarine melts.

Flavored Melted Butters

MARJORAM BUTTER:
 6 tablespoons margarine or butter
 ¼ teaspoon dried marjoram leaves
 1 teaspoon red wine

LEMON BUTTER:
 6 tablespoons margarine or butter
 1 tablespoon fresh lemon juice

DILL BUTTER:
 6 tablespoons margarine or butter
 ⅛ teaspoon dried dillweed

⅓ cup butter each

In small saucepan, melt margarine over medium heat. Stir in remaining ingredients. Cook over medium heat for 1 minute.

Orange Butter Sauce

 ½ cup margarine or butter
 ½ cup fresh orange juice
 ½ teaspoon dried thyme leaves

1 cup sauce

In small saucepan, melt margarine over medium heat. Stir in orange juice and thyme. Heat to boiling. Reduce heat. Cook over low heat 1 minute.

Zesty Tomato Sauce →

¼ cup chopped celery
2 tablespoons chopped onion
2 tablespoons margarine or butter
1 tablespoon plus 1½ teaspoons all-purpose flour
⅛ teaspoon salt
⅛ teaspoon pepper
1 can (8 ounces) tomato sauce
½ cup chili sauce
1 teaspoon sugar
1 tablespoon fresh lemon juice

1½ cups sauce

In small saucepan or skillet, cook and stir celery and onion in margarine over medium heat until tender-crisp, about 3 minutes. Stir in flour, salt and pepper. Blend in remaining ingredients. Cook, stirring constantly, until thickened, about 4 minutes.

Cocktail Sauce

1 cup chili sauce
2 tablespoons fresh lime or lemon juice
½ teaspoon prepared horseradish

1⅓ cups sauce

In small serving bowl, blend all ingredients. Chill at least 30 minutes to blend flavors.

White Wine Sauce

¼ cup finely chopped celery
1 tablespoon finely chopped onion
2 tablespoons margarine or butter
2 tablespoons all-purpose flour
⅛ teaspoon pepper
   Dash dried marjoram leaves
   Dash dried thyme leaves
¾ cup half-and-half
½ cup shredded Monterey Jack cheese
¼ cup white wine

1½ cups sauce

In small saucepan or skillet, cook and stir celery and onion in margarine over medium heat until tender, about 5 minutes. Stir in flour, pepper, marjoram and thyme. Blend in half-and-half. Cook over medium heat, stirring constantly, until thickened and bubbly, about 5 minutes. Stir in cheese until melted. Remove from heat; slowly blend in wine.

Sherried White Sauce Variation: Substitute 2 tablespoons sherry for the white wine.

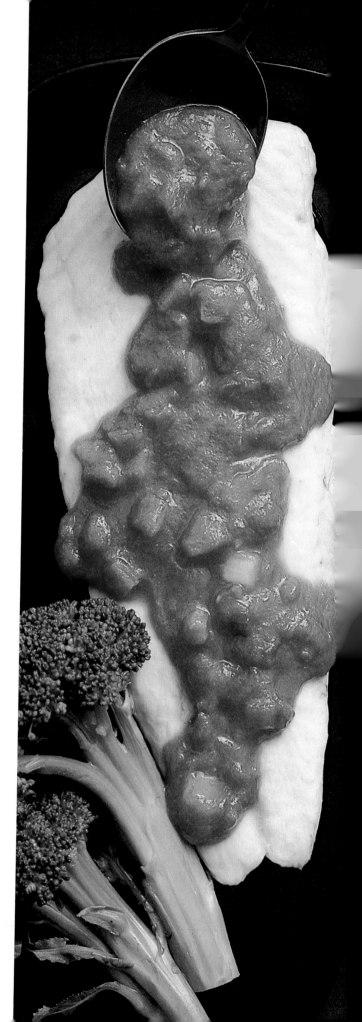

Mushroom Sauce

 2 cups chopped fresh mushrooms
¼ cup chopped onion
 2 tablespoons margarine or butter
 1 tablespoon all-purpose flour
¼ teaspoon salt
⅛ teaspoon pepper
⅓ cup milk
¼ cup dairy sour cream
 1 tablespoon Dijon-style mustard
 1 tablespoon white wine, optional

1½ cups sauce

In small saucepan or skillet, cook and stir mushrooms and onion in margarine over medium heat until onion is tender, about 5 minutes. Stir in flour, salt and pepper. Blend in milk. Cook over medium heat, stirring constantly, until thickened, about 3 minutes. Remove from heat. Stir in sour cream, mustard and wine.

Clam-Tomato Sauce

⅓ cup chopped celery
¼ cup chopped onion
 3 tablespoons margarine or butter
 1 tablespoon all-purpose flour
¼ teaspoon salt
⅛ teaspoon pepper
⅔ cup clam-tomato juice cocktail
¼ cup whipping cream
 1 tablespoon white wine

1¼ cups sauce

In small saucepan or skillet, cook and stir celery and onion in margarine over medium heat until tender, about 5 minutes. Stir in flour, salt and pepper. Blend in clam-tomato juice, cream and wine. Cook over medium heat, stirring constantly, until thickened, about 3 minutes.

Mustard Sauce

 1 tablespoon finely chopped onion
 2 tablespoons margarine or butter
 1 tablespoon all-purpose flour
¼ teaspoon salt
  Dash pepper
 1 cup milk
 2 tablespoons Dijon-style mustard

1 cup sauce

In small saucepan or skillet, cook and stir onion in margarine over medium heat for 1 minute. Stir in flour, salt and pepper. Blend in milk and mustard. Cook over medium heat, stirring constantly, until thickened, about 4 minutes.

Cucumber Sauce ↑

2 tablespoons chopped onion
1 cup chopped, seeded, peeled cucumber
2 tablespoons margarine or butter
2 tablespoons all-purpose flour
⅛ teaspoon salt
  Dash white pepper
¼ teaspoon dried dillweed
½ cup hot water
½ teaspoon instant chicken bouillon granules
½ cup whipping cream
1 egg yolk, slightly beaten

1¾ cups sauce

In 1½-quart saucepan, cook and stir onion and cucumber in margarine over medium heat until tender, about 7 minutes. Stir in flour, salt, white pepper and dillweed. Mix hot water and bouillon granules. Blend into vegetables. Stir in cream. Cook over medium heat, stirring constantly, until thickened and bubbly, about 4 minutes. Stir small amount of hot mixture into beaten egg yolk. Return to hot mixture. Cook, stirring constantly, for 1 minute.

Sweet and Sour Sauce

⅓ cup water
¼ cup sugar
¼ cup red wine vinegar
1 tablespoon plus 1½ teaspoons soy sauce
1 can (8 ounces) whole tomatoes, drained, cut up
1 small bay leaf, optional
1 medium onion, chopped
1 tablespoon cornstarch
2 tablespoons cold water

1⅓ cups sauce

In small saucepan, combine ⅓ cup water, the sugar, vinegar and soy sauce. Heat to boiling. Stir in tomatoes, bay leaf and onion. Return to boiling, stirring occasionally. Reduce heat. Simmer 5 minutes.

Blend cornstarch into 2 tablespoons cold water. Stir into sauce. Heat to boiling, stirring constantly. Cook, stirring constantly, until sauce is thickened and translucent, about 2 minutes.

143

Pickling Fish

Home-pickled fish are delicious. They are as good as, if not better than, the pickled herring sold in the grocery stores. All types of freshwater gamefish can be pickled.

Remove the heavy rib bones. If you wish, remove the skin and lateral line. Small bones can be retained, because they soften in the pickling process and can be easily eaten. Cut fish into bite-sized chunks, 1 to 1½ inches.

Use high-quality soft water in the brine solution; too much iron or sulphur adversely affects the flavor of fish. Buy bottled water, if necessary. The brine calls for pickling salt, because table salt has bitter impurities that discolor the fish and affect the taste. Use a good-quality, distilled white vinegar that has at least 5% acetic acid content. Vinegar slows spoilage.

Pickling containers include glass canning jars, glass bowls, peanut butter or mayonnaise jars. Cover containers tightly with plastic wrap or non-corrodible lids.

White onion and pimiento slices in the jars add flavor and color. The sugar and spices contribute little to fish preservation and are often adjusted to suit taste. The whole cloves add a pleasant flavor.

How to Pickle Fish

PLACE fish in the brine solution (above). Cover and refrigerate overnight. Remove; rinse in cold water and place in a glass container.

COVER fish with white vinegar and refrigerate overnight. Discard the vinegar, rinse the fish with cold water, and put it into the pickling jars.

POUR the cooled pickling solution (above) into the jars, covering the fish completely. Seal the jars. Refrigerate for 5 days before eating.

Brine Solution

1 cup pickling salt
6 cups water

In glass container, combine pickling salt and water, stirring until salt dissolves.

Pickling Solution

1 to 1½ pounds fish fillets, cut into 1-inch chunks
½ cup granulated or packed brown sugar
½ cup distilled water
1 cup white vinegar
1 tablespoon plus 1 teaspoon pickling spices
2 to 4 cloves

Mix all ingredients; heat to boiling. Reduce heat. Cover and simmer 10 to 15 minutes. Let cool to 160° to 180°F before pouring over fish.

STIR fish or shake jars once during the 5 days for good saturation. Store the undrained fish in the refrigerator no longer than 6 weeks.

SERVE pickled fish as an appetizer, snack or salad. Drain the chunks and blot thoroughly with paper towels to remove excess liquid. Serve with assorted crackers or Melba rounds. Keep the fish covered and refrigerated in the pickling solution until serving time.

147

Pickling Fish: Seviche

Seviche (pronounced *seh-veech-ee*) is a quick and easy form of pickling. The fish, which is preserved by marinating in citrus juice, is low in calories. The method is very popular in Latin America. Seviche has a limited storage life and is best when eaten within a day or two.

The best seviche is made from very fresh fish. Lean fish is usually used, though many cooks successfully experiment with oily species.

Recipe ingredients may be changed according to taste. Interesting flavors such as hot peppers, oregano, bay leaves, orange juice, soy sauce and freshly ground black pepper can be added. Lime juice has a special flavor which enhances seviche, though lemon juice can be substituted.

Seviche can be safely stored in a covered glass container in the refrigerator, though it should not be kept longer than 2 weeks.

Seviche Ingredients

1 pound very fresh lean fish fillets
½ teaspoon salt
1 medium onion, sliced
⅛ teaspoon dried oregano leaves, optional
1 small green pepper, cut into strips
3 or 4 drops hot pepper sauce
1 clove garlic, minced
3 or 4 peppercorns, optional
  Fresh lime juice

How to Prepare Seviche

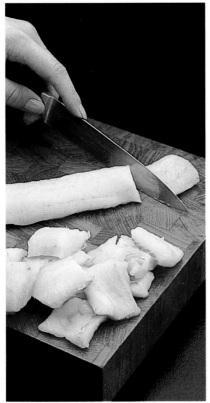

CUT skinless fillets into bite-sized chunks, 1½ inches square.

PLACE fish and the rest of the ingredients (listed above) in a glass bowl.

ADD enough lime juice so the fish is completely covered.

SERVE seviche with salt-free crackers as an appetizer or snack. Heap the fish and the vegetables on a plate of lettuce leaves and serve with crackers or hard bread as a first course salad.

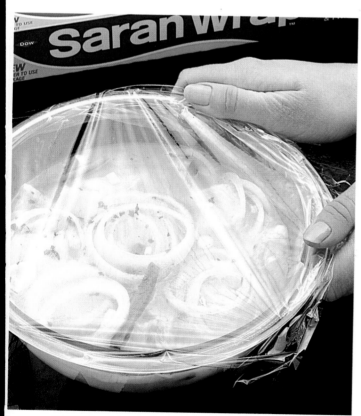

COVER with plastic wrap. Refrigerate 24 to 36 hours. The fish will lose its transparency and become firm.

DRAIN fish and vegetables before serving. To store, cover and refrigerate, undrained, no longer than 2 weeks.

Canning Fish

Home canning preserves fish for up to 1 year. It is an excellent alternative to freezing, especially when freezer space is limited. It is very useful for preserving a large catch of oily fish such as salmon, which have a short freezer life.

Fresh fillets need not be totally boneless before canning. Pressure cooking softens the bones (much like commercially canned salmon) so they can be eaten. The skin can also be retained. Smoked fish is delicious when canned; the great flavor is retained.

Home canning is easy if a few rules are followed. Use a pressure cooker because it kills bacteria during the cooking process. One-pint jars are best; fish does not cook thoroughly in quart containers. A 1-pint jar holds about 1 pound of fish.

Wash the jars and bands in hot, soapy water. After rinsing thoroughly, keep them in a sink filled with hot, clear water until you are ready to fill the jars.

How to Can Fish

SLICE the skinless fish fillets into two thin pieces if they are thicker than 1 inch. Then, cut them into 1- to 1½-inch chunks.

STUFF the fish into clean jars, allowing a ½-inch airspace. Add 1 tablespoon vinegar to each jar. With lean fish, add 1 teaspoon vegetable oil.

WIPE the jar rim thoroughly. Place the warm lid and band on the jar, and tighten them according to the lid manufacturer's directions.

Put the lids in a saucepan with hot water and place them over low heat on the stove. This will soften the rubber and the lids will seal better.

Add vinegar to the fish before canning to raise the acidity level. It is an additional safeguard against bacteria growth. Include ½ teaspoon of salt for flavor, if desired. Blend 2 teaspoons of catsup with the oil and vinegar to change the color of white fish to that of canned salmon. Dribble the mixture evenly over each layer of fish after it is placed in the jar.

After processing and cooling, check the jar seals carefully before storing. Turn the jars upside down to see if they leak. Also, use thumb pressure on the center of the lid. If the lid pops or the jar leaks, it is not sealed properly. Refrigerate and use within 2 days.

When opening canned fish, listen for the vacuum release when the lid seal is broken. Discard, *without tasting*, any fish from a jar that does not appear to be tightly sealed.

Canned fish is used as the basis of many fine dishes. Because it is already cooked, it is not as versatile as frozen fish. Canned fish can be used in fish cakes, loaf, quiche, patties, appetizers, sandwiches, salads, or any recipe calling for cooked fish. Once opened, canned fish should be drained, refrigerated and used within 2 days.

PUT the jars in the pressure cooker. Follow the instruction book for number of jars and amount of water. Process 90 minutes at 10 pounds pressure.

REMOVE the jars with tongs; place on a thick towel in a draft-free place for 12 hours. Take off bands and check seals according to lid box guidelines.

LABEL the jars. Write the fish species and canning date on freezer tape. Store the jars in a dark, cool place and use them within a year.

Salt Curing Fish: Gravlax

Gravlax originated in Scandinavia as a method of salt-curing fish. The salt draws moisture from the fish, which delays spoiling. The salt-curing process requires 4 days, but it is very easy and the finished dish is delicious.

Gravlax is usually made from salmon, though other large oily fish can be used. The fish can be either fresh or frozen.

To make gravlax, scale and fillet a 4- to 6-pound fish. Leave the skin attached. Cut the tail sections off at the vent and save them for another recipe. Use only the large fillets.

For extra flavor, substitute fresh, chopped dill for the dry dillweed. If a sweet-tasting gravlax is desired, add extra sugar to the ingredients.

Gravlax is most commonly offered as a before-dinner appetizer, though it is served for breakfast in Norway. Serve gravlax with lime juice. A sauce detracts from its unique flavor and texture.

Gravlax Ingredients

2 salmon or other oily fish fillets, 2 to 2½ pounds each, skin on
⅓ cup salt
¼ cup sugar
1 tablespoon dried dillweed
2 tablespoons coarsely ground black pepper

Mix salt, sugar, dillweed and pepper before placing on fillets. Follow photo directions.

How to Prepare Gravlax

ARRANGE one fillet, skin side down, in a glass dish. Sprinkle with ingredients (above). Place second fillet on top, thick side against thin side.

COVER the dish with aluminum foil or plastic wrap. Lay a pan or book over the entire length of the fillets. Add about 5 pounds of weight.

REFRIGERATE fish. Rearrange the weight if it shifts to one side. After 24 hours, remove from refrigerator. Take off weight and foil.

SPRINKLE lime juice on gravlax. Serve as an appetizer with crackers. If desired, spread mayonnaise on the cracker.

DRAIN the liquid and turn fillets over; replace foil and weight and refrigerate. Repeat draining and turning steps two more times, 24 hours apart.

SCRAPE the salt mixture from the flesh on the fourth day. Wrap each fillet in aluminum foil. Refrigerate no longer than 2 weeks.

PLACE the gravlax, skin side down, on a cutting board. Using a fillet knife, slice thin strips at a slight angle. Turn the knife to free flesh from skin.

Index